LANDMARK COLLECTOR'S LIBRARY

Country Houses

in Edwardian Cheshire

Compiled by Helen Maurice-Jones
from the books of Fletcher Moss

Alderley, outside a farmhouse, formerly The Eagle & Child Inn

Landmark Publishing is looking for authors

Landmark is extending its list of local books and is looking for authors of titles on Cheshire.

If you are working on a subject involving primary records or are interested in compiling a book of photographs of your town or a group of villages, taken in the 20th century, we will be pleased to hear from you.

Titles already planned include:
Historic Gardens of Cheshire
Prehistoric Cheshire

Available now:
The Spirit of Penley: The 20th Century in Photographs
The Spirit of Macclesfield: The 20th Century in Photographs
North Wales and Chester in the Civil War

Our address is on page 4.

LANDMARK COLLECTOR'S LIBRARY

Country Houses
in Edwardian Cheshire

Compiled by Helen Maurice-Jones
from the books of Fletcher Moss

Landmark Publishing

Published by

Ashbourne Hall, Cokayne Ave
Ashbourne, Derbyshire DE6 1EJ England
Tel: (01335) 347349 Fax: (01335) 347303
e-mail: landmark@clara.net
web site: www.landmarkpublishing.co.uk

1st edition

ISBN 1 84306 112 0

Printed by Bath Press, Ltd, Bath, England

Design & reproduction by Simon Hartshorne

Cover photographs

Front cover: Crewe Hall

Back cover Top: Welltrough Hall, nr Holmes Chapel
Back cover Bottom: The Bents, nr Wilmslow

Contents

For key to map see page 5

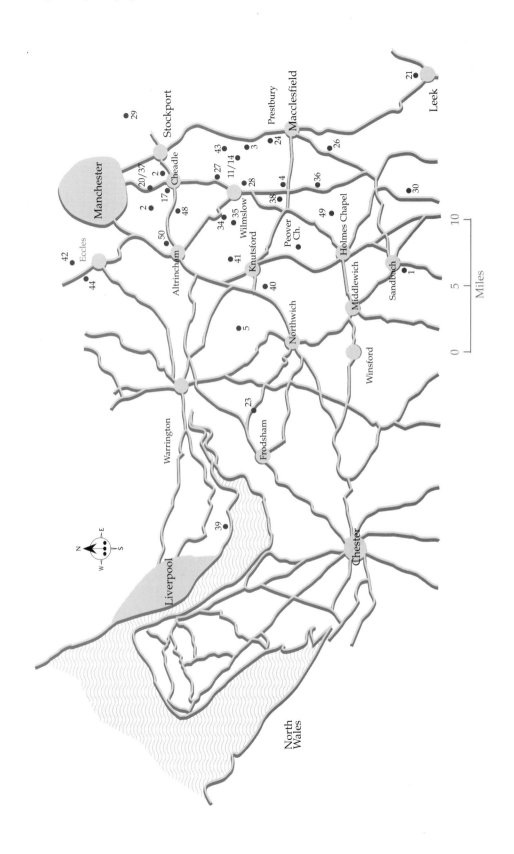

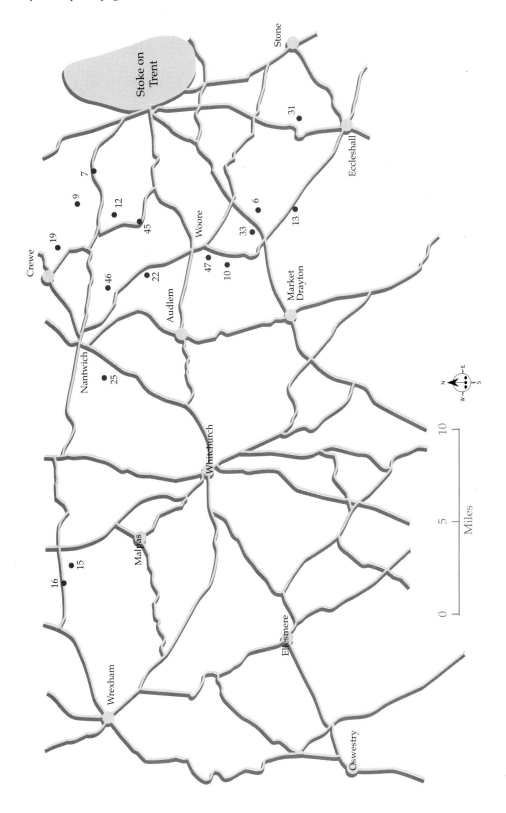

Introduction

This book brings together a collection of detailed photographs, mainly of buildings (homes, churches etc) taken in the early years of the 20th Century. This selection records journeys spanning 12 years. They were embarked upon by Fletcher Moss and his photographer companion, (referred to in the original text as Mr X), known to be a Mr James Watts.

Their wanderings, experiences and philosophy filled six volumes and contained photographs and recollections of journeys from their homes. Fletcher Moss lived at the Old Parsonage, Didsbury and James Watts at Abney Hall, nearby. They travelled to areas stretching as far as Derbyshire, the length of the Welsh Borders, parts of Somerset and also northwards to the Scottish Border.

Their excursions were made by rail and bicycle, with a determination to 'make good their spare time' by visiting buildings that interested them. They recorded by pen and picture their beauty and charm, captured as a history for us to appreciate a century later.

Fletcher Moss loved writing about his travels, which he described as pilgrimages. He had a great interest in heritage and with the help of James Watts, wanted to share this enthusiasm.

The text of this book has been cut from the original books, ignoring some of it where the author took the liberty to digress into other matters, whilst including sections which reflect his character. One can sense a wry sense of humour especially when he detected the absurd (e.g. the Rector at Gawsworth). He certainly did not have a high regard for lawyers either! In some cases illustrations were used unaccompanied by a description, although some of these have been reproduced none-the-less. Quite often, the location of a house is not as clear as it should have been.

Fletcher Moss was used to a way of life and a world which was rapidly changing. Many of these buildings will have altered, or their use will have changed. However we can be grateful to these two gentlemen for giving us an insight into the places they visited in Edwardian times.

This first book covers houses visited in and around Cheshire and will be followed by a companion volume on The Welsh Borders in 2004.

Helen Maurice-Jones, August 2003

Dorrington Hall, on the border of Shropshire with Cheshire

Abbeyfield, Sandbach

The old home that we went to see is named Abbeyfield; formerly it was the Abbot's Field, or Field House, the land having been owned in pre-Reformation times by the Abbot of Dieulacres. Some stones on a small island overgrown with trees and bushes may mark the site of the first dwelling. The present house is shown in our photograph beyond the old moat.

There is one room in it that must be duly recorded, for I should think it is

unique in our virtuous days. It is the cockpit over the dining-room. The latter is a fine room, but had been rather low. The ceiling was raised about a yard, and consequently the rooms above were spoilt, as they were then only five feet or thereabouts in height, and the late Mr. Woolf was six feet six inches, and had sons taller than himself. A large room in a country house where men could not stand upright, but could sit down secure from intrusion, was evidently well adapted to be a cockpit and there were good-looking game-birds to be seen on the premises some of them having travelled from Didsbury.

For twenty-five years a branch of the Woolf family had lived here; the old couple were dead and the next generation would not stay in the house. There had been six deaths there in their time, and others shortly before. The bit of old folk-lore about the ill-luck attending the confiscated lands of the religious houses turned up again. It may be another of my relatives lived there much further back, for I came across the following bit in a Chester paper of long ago, and though my father, John Moss, had an uncle John Moss, I cannot trace this John, who apparently left no children.

'On Monday the 21st of January 1771 (at his own
Hall formerly called Field House, near Sandbach) died
John Moss, gentleman, aged 82 years, and perfectly
sensible to the last. He was an Honest Man, a sincere
Friend, a kind Master, and a loving and peaceable
Neighbour.'

Epitaphs are said to lie like lawyers; but as there is nothing to show this eulogium was untrue, let us believe it was another instance where the hoary head is a crown of glory.

Abney Hall, Cheadle

Abney Hall, the dining room

Abney Hall was originally planned on a magnificent scale, by or for one who like many others was not able to finish. Folklorists know full well how those who build fine houses quickly end their days. In this one a corner was hurriedly made ready so that the owner might die in peace. In olden times the proverb grew, 'Fools build houses, wise men live in them;' but our modern jerry-builders are reversing that, they wax fat and softly say among themselves, 'We build houses, fools live in them.'

When Abney Hall, with its deeply sculptured stone and massive oak, was lying derelict, X's father bought it and finished it with all its details of furniture, gardens, and stables, in the sumptuous style already planned by artists in their work. During the Art Treasures Exhibition in 1857, when Sir James Watts was Mayor of Manchester, and again, in 1871 when he was High Sheriff of the County of Lancaster, the hospitality of Abney was renowned. Here came all the prominent men of the day irrespective of their politics or religion. Even Bishops pocketed their aversion to Dissenters and deigned to smile. The great rivals, Gladstone and Disraeli (at different times), brought their respective wives and stayed. Bright and Cobden, leaders of the people in their day and generation; Lord Brougham (aged 92), who had three sets of teeth, one for eating, one for sleeping, and one for talking – swore at everything and everybody; the Duke of Argyll, the Earl of Derby, Lord John Russell, Earl Granville, Monckton Milnes, Ed. Miall, W. E. Forster, and many others. At a dinner given to the Bar there were four future judges present, Lord Russell of Killowen and Lord Herschel being in company.

The greatest entertainment for the greatest number was when Prince Albert and his suite of dukes and earls stayed for some days. The Life Guards guarded the gates, to the intense admiration of all the awe-struck lads for miles around. One of Sir James's pet tales with a moral in it was to point to a motto on the ceiling of the library, 'Seest thou a man diligent in his business, he shall stand before kings,' and say the nearest approach to it he knew was that he had several times sat and chatted under that motto with Prince Albert.

All round the cornices and compartments in the ceilings of the State rooms are elaborately painted mottoes – easy ones for the entertaining rooms, but Latin for the dining-room, so that any bored diner lacking in conversation may ask his or her neighbour if they could help them with a translation. Memories are short nowadays – the answer generally is, 'I have really quite forgotten all my Latin.'

Some of the three hundred oil-paintings are historical and interesting. They include Holbein's Sir Anthony Browne, in a carved frame, with his coat of arms, pedigree, &c., on the panel. This picture came from Hengrave in Suffolk. Sir Anthony was Master of the Horse to Henry VIII, and as his proxy, married Ann of Cleves, who was so ugly that when Henry saw her he used bad language, and said Anthony could keep her. There are also pictures by Gainsborough, Ansdell, Kneller, Romney, Sant, Phillip, and many others.

For any one who may be interested in chairs there is an extraordinary collection, for in addition to sixty-six old oak chairs, most of them carved, some of them dated, there are chairs of all ages, styles, and varied woods, some of them with a little history. The rush-bottomed ones of Sam Crompton, the inventor of the machine known as 'the mule,' which revolutionised cotton-spinning, making fortunes for others but trouble for the inventor, came from Hall-i'-th'-Wood, his home near Bolton. There are hard-bottomed ones of Cardinal Manning and John Wesley; the chairs of Dr. Isaac Watts, Thackeray, Lord Byron, Liversege, and others, among them being four carved ones and a gate table all in oak, formerly used by Southey the poet.

A score of big oaken tables have come from the halls and farms all over Cheshire. The last arrival had its top of heavy worn planks all loose, while on its framework underneath is roughly carved 'H I T – IVLY 20 –1672. John Chadwick of Godley did maed this table.' Another one, dated 1677, was in Hollingworth Hall, Mottram, for two centuries, with chairs to match.

Bed from Tamworth Castle, dated 1559, Abney Hall

The reader may think I am cataloguing a museum if I mention a tithe of the curiosities in carved work, armour, ancient furniture, &c., &c., which crowd the walls at Abney. Of cabinets, chests, coffers, cupboards, or dressers, there are more than fifty. Some of them are dated with names or initials on them, most of the dates being of the seventeenth century. Of the three fine oak bedsteads, one came from Tamworth Castle. On the head is the motto 'Esto semper Fidelis' (Be thou always faithful), and at the foot is 'Feare God and Honor the Queene, 1559'. Any one could read the latter, so there would be no excuse for disobedience but perhaps the former was mercifully put in Latin, so that erring sinners might not be reproached.

The grandfathers' clocks are very numerous, for Bailey, the late steward of the manor, who lived in his thatched house on Gatley Green, and told me such wonderful tales of the folk and the folklore recorded in the Chronicles of Cheadle and Gatley was partly a clockmaker by profession as well as a cobbler. Gatley, being at the borders of two counties, in three or four parishes, and near a river, was always a lawless place, and convenient for resurrectionists, who could often make more of a dead man than ever he was worth when alive.

Sometimes they were fortunate enough to get a good oak coffin, which, if not used again, would make a grand clock case, for burial in the ground for a few years mellows and darkens the oak. Why it was customary to put the makers name on clocks but not the date, I do not know. The houses and furniture of the seventeenth century are often dated.

Among instruments of music there are a harpsichord, a spinet, and many fiddles, one of the last being marked Antonius Stradivarius, 1721.

The cap which Oliver Cromwell wore when he was a baby has finely embroidered, 'Sweet bab don't cry, 1599.' This was bought from a descendant of the Protector. St. Oliver being patron saint of the late knight. Some very costly jewelled candelabra from the sack of the Tuileries in 1848 are worth noting. For those who have a craze for china there are figures, jugs, vases, &c. &c., of Crown Derby, Delft, Sevres, Dresden, Chelsea, Nankin, Rockingham, Wedgwood, Worcester, and many other names, Oriental and Italian, that neither of us knows how to spell and much study is a weariness of the flesh.

As a fitting conclusion, let me record where an old home, or what was left of one, was bodily transported and set up again merely as a memento of the past.

The maiden name of X's mother was Buckley. The Buckleys were an old family with a small estate at Buckley Hall, near Rochdale, on the hills by the border of Yorkshire. It is possible they were distantly connected with the Bulkeleys of Cheadle Bulkeley, an ancient manor of which Abney is now the hall. The old stone house named Buckley Hall was being demolished a few years since, when X heard of it. He at once went to see it, bought what was left or could be got, numbered the stones, preserved the oaken beams, and set it up on one of the garden lawns, an original gable, with a large hall or barn behind, which is now filled with old oaken furniture, and where crowds are fed on festive occasions without turning them loose among the other treasures.

A restored remnant of Buckley Hall at Abney

The Terrace Room, Abney Hall

Still travelling on our pilgrim's way to Prestbury, every mile of this fertile country shows us some timeworn, weather-beaten house, but few have their long eventful history so graven on their many styles of building as the Hall of Adlington. Over a steep little bridge across a busy bustling river, we come to woods where, in midsummer, is a grand display of snow-white flowers several inches across and perfumed like orange blossom, lofty waving bushes of the best variety of syringas. A muffled sleepy mill is there, with old millstones outside the door, and a pool, a remnant it may be of the once useful moat. On its waters the waterhens and wild ducks splash and play, and beyond is a many-gabled red-brick house, its front to the park being built of stone, with enormous columns and inscription, classical, grand, and ugly.

Between these outer walls there is an inner house with courtyard, a gem of black and white, signed and dated, with lofty central hall, open to the heavy beamed roof, gorgeous with emblazoned heraldry.

There are very few of the old English halls that have so well escaped the ravages of time. One was built here in 1505, or, as the inscription said, 'a do MCCCCCVRRHVIIXX' – the latter part meaning in the reign of King Henry the Seventh, the twentieth year. It was rebuilt or enlarged in 1581, as the inscription over the doorway still shows, and the beautiful central hall, with its hammer-beam roof, had then 181 shields of arms of the families related to the Leghs. The display of heraldry is much less now than it was then, but it is still large and interesting. There is also an organ, on which a doubtful tradition says Handel first played 'The Harmonious Blacksmith'.

Inset above: The porch, Adlington Hall

Alderley Hall, nr. Alderley Edge

The first mention of the hall is that about 1580, Dorothy Stanley 'who liveth sole,' built or rebuilt a house, which Sir Thomas Stanley greatly enlarged about 1630, and which Sir Edward Stanley added to in 1754. But in March 1779, nearly all was burnt, and it has never been rebuilt. A noted portrait, by Gainsborough, of the first lord's father, was too big for removal, and perished with other treasures. The spacious courtyard where the village forces mustered in the times of danger, and the central hall where harvest home was feasted, when the oldest servant Peter danced the Cheshire round with Charlotte Allcock on the high table, are all gone.

For above a hundred years potatoes and onions have flourished on part of the site of this old home. The ancient mounting-block still stands by the bridge, though pillions are no more, and ornamental pillars of stone are picturesquely awry after three centuries of storms. Even since these words were written and photographs taken, another stone column has fallen with the weight of years and ivy. What a wonderful thing it is that so near to our bustling, restless city of Manchester, there is to-day a house where you might take a plunge from your bedroom window and paddle about for your morning bath among the ducks and fishes; or fish from your window for your breakfast as you are dressing or listen as you lie in bed to the lap, lap, lapping of the water on the walls, or the gentle rustle of the ripples in the reeds, while you lazily dream of the days of love and long ago.

The beech trees were grown from beechmast brought from Kyre, in Worcestershire whence the Sir Thomas Stanley of that day had brought his wife. The date would probably be from about 1630 to 1650. A great grandson of the above planted firs on the Edge about 1750, and in 1797, Sir John Thomas Stanley, the first lord, wants 'hundreds of bushels of seeds of forest trees for the further decoration of Alderley.' The love of trees, and the care of the estates, seem to have been a family inheritance which survived their many changes of religion and politics.

Alderley Hall showing the moat

This farm house in Alderley, previously the Eagle and Child Inn,
was still selling soft-drinks when this photograph was taken.

Lane to the church, Alderley

Above: Clock House, Alderley Edge. Below: Alderley Mill

Arley Hall

Arley Hall is about six miles to the south of the place whence the family take their name. By the lane side at High Legh are ancient stocks where for the first time X tries what he might have had to try if he had lived in the olden time, and had not always been so good. Behind the fence, embowered in splendid trees, on the margin of a wide-spreading lawn, where wave the plumes of pampas grass, there stands another curious old chapel. This has been restored recklessly, not in the cheap and ugly manner that is common, but reckless as to cost and magnificence. Wonderfully carved oak all around, with choir stalls, rood screen and cross, many-tinted glass both old and new, and fount inlaid with showy marbles. One old window, or part of it, does commemorate the founder, Thomas Legh, of High Legh, and his wife Isabella, the heir of Trafford of 'Garet' (Manchester), with their arms emblazoned on their mantles, the date being 1581. The whole place is very small but very grand. It is virtually in the garden of the East Hall. Some one has evidently very high and ornate tastes and the means to gratify them. A priest in the garb of a monk even to cassock and sandals comes in, but he does not look as if he mortified the flesh.

'In Cheshire, Leghs are thick as fleas'. Here at High Legh we are in the midst of them. Those at East Hall are Leghs; at West Hall, Leighs. There are any amount of branches up and down the country. Common folk, who spell their names Lee or Lea, may even be humble relations, but if any one wishes to harmlessly insult one of the reigning houses they should spell their name in the way it should not be spelt.

A little farther down the lane we come to the first of the rhyming signposts:

'This road forbidden is to all
Unless they wend their way to call
At mill or green or Arley Hall'.

As we have the autograph of the Squire in our pocket we go down this forbidden road, although it needs very careful steering, for big stones are placed on it at various angles. At the mill is a pedlar who wants to take his cartload of very miscellaneous merchandise still farther, and says he ' mun ar brass from someweers.' When we tell him he has dropped some of his baskets in the lane he swears at large and curses all things. Perhaps the poor old mule will suffer for it, but what could he hope to sell at the stately hall of Arley?

The Green is like one of those fancy greens we see in picture-books or on Christmas cards. It is a large space of beautiful greensward where the children can play on real grass, climb real trees, and tumble into real water, for the mere extends from the mill past the green and on towards the hall, perhaps a mile in length. The school-house has been made out of one of the big old barns, with great oak timbers and heavy grey slates on the roof. The adjoining houses have been built to look alike. All are now clad in ivy, jessamine, or clematis, and there are actually wagtails and fly-catchers nests on the very walls and roof of the school. I can testify to the nests; some of them had squalling youngsters in, which would be very disturbing to the poor boys at their lessons. I once found fault with a boy (the son of a servant) for not doing something he had been told to do, and his excuse was that he always forgot except when he was in school, and then they would not let him go to do it.

lt is not known when the Warburtons settled at Arley; but in 1360 Galfrido de Werburghton had a licence for an oratory there, so it is almost certain a hall existed previously. In 1469 'Wise' Piers, or Peter, rebuilt the hall and chapel. This Piers was a retainer of the Stanleys, and probably,

Gatehouse to stable-yard, Arley

like his overlords, got richer after the Bosworth fight. His son John was 'the mighty Warbartone out of Chesshire,' mentioned in a poem on Flodden. The new hall of Peter was quadrangular, timber built, and surrounded with a moat, as was the custom in those days. Its great hall still exists within the present one. In 1758 this picturesque and beautiful old house was encased with common brick, and spoilt of course, although in Ormerod's time the quad enclosed a court, round which there was an open colonnade decked with parterres of flowers. Then in 1833 all was demolished, and the present house, stately and grand, arose in its stead.

Above & opposite: Arley School, Arley Green

Top: Arley Mill. Bottom: The ancient timber-framed barn at Arley

The Parsonage, Ashley, just over the border into Staffordshire

Staffordshire is lamentably lacking of histories. There are fine old halls at Audley and Betley, but I cannot find any mention of them in any book. The date that some one has painted on the ruined hall of Audley is probably taken from a charter of Henry III confirming many lordships or manors to Henry de Alditheleighe in 1227. The charter mentions a new hall, but this Henry de Audeley, who had great estates, built a castle at Heley and got a license for a market at Betley, or Bettelegh as it was then spelt. The hall at Audley may have been rebuilt about 1540 as it bears another date.

The first mention of the name that I find was Liulf de Aldithelee, who murdered Gamel, son of Griffith, thane of Betley. Gamel was a common name with the Saxons or English, but Griffith is British or Welsh, and many Audleys in after years were slain by the Welsh. The blood-feud probably lasted, for the high ley on its steep hill became a border fortress.

Baguley Hall

As the lovely weather of early June became more hot and sultry we one fine day set forth from Didsbury to cycle calmly along, and photograph more of the picturesque halls in the neighbourhood.

Baguley Hall, in its central part, is a grand specimen of the great halls of our forefathers. The oak trees, or sections of them, which frame it are of enormous size, some of them being reversed and five or six feet in diameter. Only earthquakes or explosions can damage these, for fire, storm, and tempest have long been tried. In the hall rests the effigy of Sir William de Baguley, with his Baguley shield of arms. It was in Bowdon Church for centuries, and then desecrated and stolen to deck a churchwarden's garden, but is now returned to the hall where

'At Bagily that bearne
His biding place had,
And his ancestors of olde time
Have yearded there longe.
Before William Conquerour
This country did inhabitt.
Jesus bringe them to blisse
That broughte us forth of bale.'

Poetic licence does not trouble about truth. It makes assertions with more or less truth, and calmly defies contradiction. The knightly family of Baguley seem to have enjoyed the manor from whence they took their name for only a short time. Some of them may have bided or herded or yarded there long, but the name and family did not flourish, and in America, where the 'Biglow Papers' are well known, the Bigelows or Big-lows claim to be the Baguleys of Baguley, for they, having piled up their wealth, have naturally sought after their ancestors and arms. We with resigned amazement learn that the Baguleys of Baguley emigrated to America long years before that great continent was discovered, and in the New World restored the fallen fortunes of their famous house.

From the hall we went by Longhurst Knowl or Knoll – the rounded hill from which the valley of the Mersey may be seen from its source to the sea – to Baguley Lodge, a thatched house built on part of the ancient waste or moor of Baguley, where the new Sanatorium for the Withington district is to be built. It was time to photograph the old house ere it fell or its beauty was destroyed, for its thatch was perishing, its floors were rotting, and over the portals where Ichabod should be written was a mouldering shield of arms.

The oaken roof of Baguley Hall

Baguley Hall with the effigy of Sir William de Bagulegh on the right

Barlow Hall

The newer end of Barlow Hall

Strictly speaking, Barlow seems never to have been anything but a hall and a moor. It was neither parish nor township, and yet there are several records where mention is made of the lordship and manor of Barlow. The hall was the home of one eminent family for four hundred years. An intensely conservative family; more than one of whose members sacrificed everything, even to life itself, for their faith. The moor that extended for two miles from near the hall to Didsbury seems to have been named Diddesbury Moor a long time ago, but in later years Barlow Moor. Where the moor lane joined the main road at Didsbury there grew up a colony of shops and small houses which we called Barlow Moor. But a railway was made there, and the station labelled Didsbury.

Then houses sprang up from the ground as the mushrooms suddenly come with the warm dews of autumn. Miles of streets soon covered the site of the moor; the "bare low" of Barlow. There are now about 10,000 people, where fifty years ago were 1,449. At the beginning of the 19th century there were 619, and now we have more than that number in the workhouse, so greatly have we advanced. The names of the districts or places have been changed. The residuary parish of Didsbury is small and select, the church has been 'thoroughly restored' several times in my life, and the Barlow Chapel has utterly vanished as though it ne'er had been, so complete has been the restoration.

It is a wonder that Barlow Hall has not vanished also, but it is in a secluded, lonesome part of the old moor, and near to the river Mersey. It is now two or three hundred yards outside the boundary of Didsbury township, being included in Chorlton-cum-Hardy. Just three hundred years ago there were lawsuits about the manorial rights and encroachments on the waste grounds of the moors of Didisburye and Chollerton or Chowreton, the Barlows of Barlow Hall being complained of.

The oldest deed of which I can find any record about Didsbury or Barlow rather curiously refers to both places. As there is no date to it, it was probably made before AD 1300. Alexander and Roger were always common names in the Barlow family, and some members were generally priests. This one was evidently wealthy, and, being in the church, settled his property on family relatives. From abstracts of family deeds in the Harleian MSS it appears: 'Alexander, the chaplain ('cap'lnus') of Didsbury, settles all his lands in Barlow, Chollerton, Harday, and the water mill, on Roger de Barlow, his son Thomas, and all lawful heirs.'

In 1397 a certificate from Lichfield, beginning 'In Dei noie, Amen' (In the name of God, Amen), says that Thomas de Barlow is the sole lord of Barlow, there having apparently been the usual litigation. Skipping over a few more years let us notice that twice on the present house is the date 1574. On the dial on the wall is written 'Lumen me regit 1574 vos umbra' (The light rules me, the shade rules you). There may be some reference here to the frequent changes of faith which were then common.

In what is sometimes called the chapel window, a fine old window which faces the east, there is the same date, the initials A. B., several shields of arms, the Earl of Derby's being one, and the mottoes 'Prist en Foyt' and 'Respice finem'. These mottoes appear to have been used as guides, constancy in faith to the end.

Shortly after the rebuilding of the house, namely in 1584, it was searched for priests. It may have been thought there were too many hiding-holes or secret chambers wanted in it, and that it had been altered for that purpose. No priests were found, but the master was dragged to prison in Manchester, where he soon afterwards died, and was buried at Didsbury. The registers record 'Alexander Barlowe de Barlowe, esquyer.' His son, Sir Alexander, in his will said, 'Yf yt fortune I die within twentye myles of my house of Barlowe, that my sayd bodye be leyde in Didsburye

Overleaf: The Courtyard at Barlow

Churche, as neere unto my father as may be,' but they buried him by torchlight at Manchester. This Sir Alexander was married at four years old, renounced that wife, and married the daughter of Sir Uryan Brereton, of Honford, by whom he had fourteen children. His picture has been often engraved. One of his sons was Rudesind, the President of the English Benedictines, and a more famous one was Edward the Martyr.

Barlow Hall from the lake

Barthomley

This parish suffered an appalling tragedy during the Civil War. It was on Christmas Eve 1643, the anniversary of the angels song of 'peace on earth good will to men,' a troop of Royalists came to Barthomley when unarmed Roundheads were in the church. Christmas was not Merry Christmas then, for the soldiers of 'God and the King' cut the throats of twelve of the Puritans, stripped their bodies, and left them. Two of them were named Steele, and were probably from Sandbach. The names of others are in my book on Folk-Lore.* The church registers of the date are mutilated, for the parson told me the massacre was done by 'the wrong side.'....

I could have told them a tale that was told to me fifty years ago about the host of the White Lion at Barthomley, but as the present tenants may be his descendants I kept quiet and will tell it now, merely premising that the house bears the initials O.H, is dated 1614, and is believed to have always been an inn. It had to be propped up when we were there, as if it were soaked in its own liquor.

In the days when the clerk of the church kept the village inn and his feudal tenure or polygenous duties comprised the carting of his rector's coals, he went to Audley coal-pits for a load of coal, and took a barrel of ale with him. He would naturally be fresh, and he was persuaded to have more, was taken down the coal-pit when the drink had overcome him, and there he was left in the darkness. When his muddled senses returned and the colliers gibed at him, he cried aloud: 'Oh please, good master devils, don't hurt me. I never hurted nobody. When I was on earth I was clerk of Barthomley; now I'm what you please.' As he was only drunk and kept an ale-house when he was on earth they let him loose.

Folk Lore, Old Customs, and Tales

Left: The White Lion, Barthomley. Above: Barthomley Church

The Bents, nr. Browne's House*

Behind Browne's House is another one much older, with a most picturesque projecting dormer window. Wattle and daub protrudes between the massive oaken timbers – hazel rods and bents daubed with clay, impervious to any weather. This ancient cot is tumbling to decay, as it has been for centuries. Shepsters build in the roof, while swallows flit around, and the house seems made for the birds. A cheery, cherry-faced old woman shows us how clean it is inside, and all so charmingly artistic, as is the old name, *The Bents*.

* See page 46

Betley Village

Broughton Hall, Staffordshire

Over Ashley Heath, by the Loggerheads inn, and through the Burnt Woods we come to Broughton, in Staffordshire. The place consists of a hall and a church. The only bit of history that I can find is in Erdeswick, *where a charter of Edward I mentions Roger de Napton, who had issue Elias de Broughton and ten generations. Their feudal duties were to plough in winter, to reap in harvest, and to keep ward at Eccleshall Castle for their overlords – the diet of a man being then valued at half-a-penny a day. The church is one of the best kept – unrestored and unmolested – little churches that I know. I painted a picture of it fifty years ago, and it looks just the same as it did then excepting for a white cross that someone has put up like the stock article of suburban cemeteries. There may have been more burials than one in the fifty years, but perhaps the other parties, the buried and the buriers, have been content with the green grass under the sod, the sweetly scented, slowly mouldering sod.

The Hall is dated 1639, [the photograph clearly shows 1637, see overleaf) and the initials T. B. over the front door stand for Thomas Broughton the builder, who had been High Sheriff of the county. His son, or grandson, would be the Sir Brian Broughton who married the heiress of the Delves of Doddington and with their descendants the estates have descended unto this day.

The Hall was built in a troublesome time at the beginning of the great Civil War. It was made with a remarkable hiding-hole – a fair-sized room with no window or aperture but a passage that branched from the main chimney flue. It seems to me that all access to this room would be cut off if the fire in the hall were lighted. To get into this hidden chamber a man would have to climb up steps in the chimney for eighteen feet, then go down a dark passage groping his way and patiently wait in the silence and gloom of the grave. If a fire was lighted after the fugitive had got safely into the secret room the smoke should ascend the chimney flue, but if the chimney 'smoked' it might be very uncomfortable. The room has now become a smoking-room with a window and stairs of its own.

The handsome staircase in the Hall does not show itself in the photograph as well as it should. We also do not attempt to give a picture of the Flemish stained glass in the hall window, though it is dated 1651, for the lady of the house showed us the figure of a rabbi about to operate with a fearful pair of scissors.

We are told the outside of the house is of timberwork, very ornamental, but unfortunately covered with plaster. The corbels are carved into the likeness of birds and beasts, and probably there are quatrefoils in black and white hidden behind the stucco.

Roundabout, in beautiful undulating parkland, are fine old trees and a gem of a little church that is good enough to have inspired Gray's *Elegy*.

* *History of Staffordshire*

The front door, Broughton

Close-up of the Hall, its facinating carved front covered with plaster

Fireplace at Broughton

Broughton Hall: the staircase

Near Newton Hall and Newton Heath is a yew, clipped into formal shape or want of shape, an arbour below, an arm-chair above. Robust and tall, though not in its prime, its age may be taken to be a little over that of the adjoining house, a squarely, solidly built house, roofed with tons of massive stone, and dated 1702. One John Browne built himself an abode, signed and dated it in a proper manner. He made no boast of heraldry, and merely indulged in a useless *e* after his name. It reminds one of an old tale about rooks, who are such staunch Conservatives that they always make their nests and noise about the house of the richest man in the parish. They have been known to desert a rookery when some new-fledged Radical has come to in-

habit the ancestral hall round which their nests were built.

Once upon a time the old squire was dead, and a dreadful rumour got spread about that some people named Smith were coming to the hall. The rooks were greatly perturbed, not knowing whether to leave at once or not, but an old patriarch advised delay, and kept close watch until he saw the luggage coming, and the amount of it showed there was wealth, and therefore the chance of getting some of it or its proceeds. The labels showed that the name of the new family was spelt with a y and an *e* at the end – Smythe, not common Smith. Their dignity, therefore, was satisfied, and the sanctimonious gentry in black went on with their egg-sucking, potato-stealing and other sins.

John Browne built his house well, with good oaken staircase and massive beams. Now there are holes in the roof and the tenant has notice to quit, though he was born there, and has lived there more than half a century. Some of us, even in these electric days, like to hear of any one living in one house, content, for fifty or more years.

In the south of Cheshire, on the lower range of the Broxton hills, midway between the picturesque little towns of Holt and Farndon on the river Dee, and the high village of Harthill on the hill of Bickerton, there stands in charming scenery another of the black-and-white houses for which the country is famous.

On one of our first pilgrimages we had seen Carden from the road, and had rested and photographed in the very quaint, old-fashioned inn known as The Cock at Barton, which is near to it. Now we asked for leave to visit the Park, and certainly the approach up a long avenue of well-grown trees, with glistening mere on one side and craggy hills on the other, is very fine. It is a case of disenchantment as we draw nearer to the large house at the end of the grand trees to find it is rather a painted sham. However the other side is genuinely timber-built, level with a garden and wide lawn, where again the trees show health and vigour, as if the soil and climate both were good.

The first syllable of the name shows its Celtic origin. It has been spelt in many ways. One family has held the place or part of it for nearly five hundred years. For the last of the Cardens left his estates to his four daughters, and Elenor married a Leche, who was probably a son of the Leech or Surgeon to King Edward III, who granted him £10 a year out of the mills on the Dee.

John le Leche succeeded John, until the pedigrees say there were fourteen Johns and only one

47

William, whose elder brother John had died without succeeding. There seems little to note in the history of the house or family, but from Malbon's diary of the Civil War, I make the following interesting extract:

'On Saturdaye, the x. of June, 1643, some Companyes marched furthe to Carden and sett upon Mr. Leeches howse (a Comissioner of Arraye), whoe did oppose theim. But in the end they gott the howse; apprehended him broughte him with theim prsonr pludred his howse; kild a servant maid with shootinge att the howse and broughte with him some others and some horses alsoe to Namptwiche'.

Some time before there had been a bear bait at Carden, when one 'Phillip Cappur, of Clutton, dyd suddenly at that disordered Sport.'

Malbon's diary is one of those invaluable histories that shortfully and truthfully give us, in old-fashioned language and spelling, a good insight into what was really done, and what folk and their homes of the time were like. The better known diary of Burghall is merely an altered plagiarism of it. Malbon was a lawyer of Nantwich and steward to the Crewe estates. He would probably be descended from Malbedeng, Baron of Wich Malbank, as Nantwich was formerly named. One of the last of the family, who was a connection of my own, changed his name to Melbourne, but the country folk still pronounced it Morbon. Malbon's own spelling is interesting to me, for it shows the local pronunciation of names was the same then as it is now. For instance, Shrewsbury is always Shrowesbury, Cholmondeley is Cholmley, Ruthin is Wrythen, Levison is Lewson.

Cock O' Barton Inn, Barton

We journey on to the Cock at Barton. This is the model of a good old-fashioned inn. We ride into the yard, and enter by the back door into a kitchen – a large timber-framed thatched building, open to the roof, with a fireplace built round with bricks in the middle of the room. It is a good untouched specimen of the rough buildings of two or three centuries ago. Previously to the manufacture of bricks, which in country districts were not common until about two or three hundred years since, on account of the scarcity of fuel, there would have been no chimney. The smoke would have had to wind its way out of the room wherever and whenever it best could get out. The taproom is also quaint, with a heavy oaken beam over the ingle nook, on which are the arms of Leche of Carden. The parlour is filled with first-rate, genuine, old oaken furniture, which is quite a treat to see.

Cheadle Moseley Hall is the ancient timber building in a field to the left of the road to Stockport, and its predecessor, or Cheadle Savage Hall, when the Savages owned their share of the manor, was possibly part of the old fold-like-looking black and white house to the right of the road to Wilmslow.

Cheadle Church

Cheadle village, from the green towards the church

Cheadle Moseley Hall

Chorley Hall, Wilmslow

By Th' Ryleys Lane we went to Chorley Hall, a quaint and curious home. Within a stone-bridged moat is half a stone-built house, with pointed Gothic doorways, dim religious light, and windows with mullions of stone. The front is to the bridge, to the left, in the accompanying picture. At right angles to it the other half of the house is timber and daub, adorned with quatrefoils, and mellowed with age. This contains an oaken panelled room with grotesque mysterious carvings, and here it is said the great Oliver once came for consultation.

Under the fir-trees at Soss Moss we ate apples and sought for the black and white hall which stands close by the railway between Alderley and Chelford, of which several beautiful photographs were made. Its huge stone lichen-clothed chimney is signed and dated 'T Wyche, 1583'

Crewe Hall, Crewe

Crewe has been the name of a hall and the name of a family for centuries, though the hall and the family name have had to be renewed more than once. It is also the name of one of the greatest railway-stations in the world, though that well-known junction of railroads really was in the neighbouring parish of Monks Coppenhall. Fortunately the powers that were gave to it the more euphonious name of Crewe. The junction of the lines from Manchester and from Liverpool on their way to London, that is now the main line of the London and North-Western Railway Company, was originally planned to be at the ancient town of Nantwich. However greedy lawyers were too grasping, and to circumvent them the junction was made a little further away, where land was cheap – cold clay soil, growing nothing but rushes and sour grass, some of the poorest land in Cheshire.

It is said that seven acres of this poor land were given to the railway company for engineers works, repair-shops, store-sheds, &c., and on those seven acres in Monks Coppenhall began the enormous engineering works that began the town of Crewe. The speculative donor (or cheap seller) had other acres of surrounding land, on which he built endless rows of workmen's dwellings, the only dwellings for miles for a constantly increasing stream of well-paid artisans. He had cast his bread upon the waters – or in more homely language, had thrown a sprat to catch a whale – to some purpose, and wisdom decreed that the whole town should bear the name of Crewe.

By the side of Crewe Green, where two worn-out cottages stood, came the junction of converging lines and a very little station. The bewildering station with its bewildering maze of lines of rails, the enormous workshops, and the prosperous town have all been built in my lifetime. It is little more than twenty years since I asked a man who had been born near to Crewe, and had long lived in Manchester, which was the way to somewhere from Crewe Station. His answer astonished me, for he said he had never been to Crewe since the railway was made. He was one of the old-fashioned sort who did not like "the new fangled" travelling. Long before motor-cars were invented I have known many who would never travel by rail if they could go by road.

Creu was the spelling of the place-name in Domesday, and the spelling was good enough for most folks. Various families owned the manor. Sir Robert Fowleshurst, one of the four famous squires of Poictiers, won it by marriage. My last book [Book four] tells of his exploits, and shows his effigy in the Crewe chapel at Barthomley with his hands clasped in prayer, clad in complete armour, and his forehead engraved with the name of his captain in the last great fight the world is to know. [*Publisher's note*: this book was written before 1914.] Another of his name fell at Flodden, and the family died away. In 1608 a successful lawyer, in the troublous times that lawyers fatten on, bought the estate, and said he was descended from the Crewes of Crewe. The local rhymer said –
'Sir Randle Crewe, the lord of the manor,
Was born at Nantwich the son of a tanner.'

Both of the tales may be true. It would not be worth anyone's while going to law with a lawyer about such a trifle. When bear-baiting was one of the sports at our local wakes, a man who had a crocodile offered to let it be baited by anyone's dogs for six-pence, but the wise men of the village agreed that to bait a crocodile would be like going to law with a lawyer.

In 1614 Ranulphe Crewe was elected Speaker of the House of Commons, and addressed the King in such a " fitting" and fulsome speech, as to His Gracious Majesty's descent from Solomon, or someone far beyond William the Conqueror, that he was soon knighted and made Kings

Serjeant-at-Law. He must have been hard-faced to touch on the Kings pedigree at all, for the blowing up of the King's father was in the memory of those present, and the mother's share in it, with other romantic episodes, could not be forgotten.

From the Journal of the House of Commons is taken the following quaint description of Mr. Crewe's election

'5 *Aprilis,* 12 *Jacobi,* 1614.

"About Twelve of the Clock, my Lord High Admiral, Lord High Steward for this Time, came into the Room commonly called the Whyte hall or Court of Requests . . . Oaths of Supremacy and Allegiance to be taken . . . attend His Majesty in the Higher House.

"At their Return (about Half an Hour past Four a Clock) Mr. Secretary Winwood, after great Silence in the House, stood up, and made a Speech, the Sum whereof was:

"That the Honour of the King and Happiness of the Subject depended upon this Parliament: Great Care therefore to be had for Choice of the Speaker now – the Speaker the Pilot to guard this great Ship.

"On all Sides great Variety of Choice for that Service; but commendeth to them specially Mr. R. Crew, for his Learning, Judgment, Religion.

"A general Voice, 'Mr. Crew.' Nemine contradicente. Mr. Crew after Silence, disableth himself by his own Infirmities; the Weight of the Business, by the Judgment of the House, by the Difficulty of the Negotiation between a Prudent King and intelligent House – Not inured to the publick Service – Never but in One Parliament – Few Observations: sithence then forgotten – Prayeth a new Choice.

"Mr Chancellor – That his Excuse Kindleth the Desire of the House to him: His Modesty specially commended.

"With a general Applause called on: and therefore fetched to the Chair by Mr. Chancellor and Mr. Secretary Winwood.

"Who still excusing himself by his Disabilities desireth Leave of the House to appeal to His Majesty for sparing him and for a better Choice."

They knew how to humbug one another even in those primitive times, for the whole programme had been arranged beforehand, and Mr. Crewe spread the butter more thickly than his rivals. He got into temporary disgrace shortly after by having a woman hanged for being a witch on the false witness of a boy who was said to be bewitched. Lawyers generally prefer the law to take its course rather than justice should be done, and the parsons would joyfully quote 'Thou shalt not suffer a witch to live': for witchcraft is against religion. What would happen to the boy or to those who prompted him? Would he say he was 'so sorry' or would he 'stick to it'? Would he be taken by the angels to Abraham's bosom or go with Dives to the other place?

Sir Ranulphe's fortune was made, and he began to build a grand new hall at Crewe. It took twenty one years to build, and was finished just in time for the Civil War.

In 1625 Sir Ranulphe Crewe was made Lord Chief Justice of England, but the next year he was turned out of his office by the new King, Charles I, for he sided with the people against the illegal and arbitrary demands of the King for the levying of 'ship' money and the seizing of those who refused to pay.

There were many petitions for his restoration to his high office, but Charles would never tolerate anyone who thought for himself. The old man lived on in retirement for twenty years, and the latter part of the time in poverty. His great savings had been invested in the estate and swallowed in the new hall. When the Civil War began, with its great demands upon him, he said, 'I myself

The drive to Crewe Hall

The garden front

The Hall with its gates

receive nothing of my revenue, and have been plundered to a great value. . . I know not how to supply but upon credit the means of my subsisting, and I hope my credit shall not fail. . . Would to God mine eyes might be closed in the days of peace.'

Peace! 'Peace on earth, goodwill to men.' The Christmas Eve of the massacre at Barthomley had just passed, the bodies of the villagers were scarce cold in their graves, and here is a bit from the diary of Malbon of Nantwich: 'A Garrison putt into the Hall of Crewe for the p'liam^t ptie. The Kinges forces laide great Seige agaynst the same howse And on St. Johns Daye in Christmas 1643 they in the howse slewe from the howse about three score of the Kinges ptie and wounded many: but the Kinges forces encreasinge to a very greate number And Namptwiche not able to releave them and they in the howse wantinge both victualls and Amunycon vpon Innocents daye att Nighte not able to houlde out any longer and p'ceyvinge noe Aide comynge to theim (althoughe as valyant Soldyers as any weire) weire enforced to yeld upp the howse and theimselves prsoners to the Kinges ptie; havinge quarter gyven theim and being in theire custodie (to the nu'ber of one hundred or more) weire all putt prsoners into the stable and afterwards putt into Betley churche.'

Sir Ranuphe was living at his house at Westminster at the time, and would not hear of the bloodshed at his grand new hall until the fighting there was over. The Royalists retired strategically when Sir Thomas Fairfax, as General of Cheshire, made his quarters in Crewe Hall with four hundred men, the soldiers lying on straw in the great hall, making themselves as much at home as they could, and not particular as to the wood that made the fires burn. The old man died at Westminster aged eighty-six, and five months after was buried in the Crewe chapel at Barthomley.

A big new vault had to be made, and the bones could not he moved from Westminster until the Speaker gave permission.

After the flurry and the fury of the Civil War were done a stagnant peace fell upon the land, when our taste in all things was the vilest ever known. The friends of Crewe Hall wrecked it worse than its foes had done. The great stone gateway ornamented with Sir Ranulphe's arms and motto, the lozenge-patterned path across the forecourt, the terraces and balustrades, the old-fashioned flower garden with its trim parterres, were all swept away. Down went garden walls, outhouses, and offices, until the hall could stand in its majesty in the park alone, according to the taste of the day. Then another architect proposed to make the house itself look stately and new by plastering it all over, so that at a distance it should seem to be built of stone. The outside escaped that churchwarden-decoration, but the grained and carved oak of the interior was bedaubed with "pleasant" paint to make it look more cheerful, and the panelled bedrooms were papered with fashionable paper.

Lords, gardeners, and architects flourished, faded, made their little alterations, and passed away: generations of them, most of them wise in their own conceit; and new men came with new ideas, many of their new ideas being the old ideas in another guise. They went in for restoration, and all that art and wealth could do to retain the old house with its surroundings in accordance with its style was lavishly done. But – in one night it perished. On the night of New Year's Day 1866 fire consumed the greater part.

In the morning, from a table on the grass plot, Lord Crewe sent an urgent message to Barry the architect to come at once and begin the very necessary restoration once again. In a few years an archbishop consecrated the rebuilt old home, and that is the house here shown.

The best has been made of a situation as flat and uninteresting as any in Cheshire, though it is rising to the Staffordshire border. The grand new gates to the forecourt have plainly written across them in big letters of gold, 'QVID RETRIBVAM DOMINO' ('What can I retribute (or render) to the Lord?'), and at the base of the steps to the front door a sejant-rampant lion holds a scroll, "Quid retribuam Domino"; up and down the place other beasts present the same question, and over the hearth as you sit at the fire, you may ponder the same problem, 'What can I render to the Lord'?

It is not the Crewe motto, for that is "Sequor nec inferior," as may be seen on the chimney-piece of the drawing-room, but it is a much better one, especially when multiplied by the numerous heraldic monsters that deck the terraces and gardens. Fearful and wonderful

Right: The front terrace

wildfowl some of them are, but they are very picturesque, and greatly enliven the walks round the house.

There is a magnificent display of heraldry all over the place, but unfortunately we had no one to interpret it. The lion on the right hand at the bottom of the stairs holds the shield of Done of Utkynton, the unicorn holds the lion of Crewe. The enormous shield of Arms seems to me and a fellow-student to have come from Utkynton, or perhaps been copied from a great shield of Sir John Crewe's in Tarporley Church. Sir Ranulphe's second son John became Crewe of Utkynton when he married the heiress of the Dones, and his son Sir John would be entitled to quarter the Done arms, but that branch of the Crewes died out. The shield with Crewe and Offley quarterings would be the proper one for the late Hungerford Lord Crewe, and it is to be seen in many places all over the house. The number and variety of other shields glowing in all the splendour of the rainbow at every window, skylight, electric light, or wherever light can show the gorgeous tinctures, is wonderful – enough to dazzle and satiate the tired eyes of antiquaries bewildered.

It would be useless for me to attempt to explain the elaborate embellishments of this grand house, the intricate patterns on the ceilings, the carved figures, plaques, sculpture; whatever they may be that are in medallions on the cornices, marbles of many colours, alabaster, onyx and jasper in the mantelpieces, and gorgeous work everywhere.

The only room that escaped the fire is shown. It is called "His Lordship's room," and its dark oaken panelling looks rather solemn after seeing its glowing neighbours. Hinchlifle says the oak pillars that supported the roof of the central hall in his day, all emblazoned with armorial bearings, had been taken out of the stalls of the old stables; and he says that 'sages' have never settled what was meant by the allegorical device on the chimney-piece in the dining-hall. An extraordinary female plays the goddess with stick or sceptre, and a bunch of grapes. She triumphs over fighting men, drunken bears, horses kicking one another, and many wondrous things. Perhaps it was meant for 'Good Queen Bess' enjoying herself.

Another room with a wonderful chimney-piece shows Cain killing Abel, about the size of life. It is a bedroom, and any one who tries to sleep in it with that ghastly murder in grey plaster haunting him, should be uncommonly good.

All the glories of the carved parlour, the great gallery with its pictures by famous artists of famous men, the library, and other grand rooms we must hurriedly pass, if anything is to be said of those who here lived and died....

Right: The front door

59

Through the library to the drawing room

*The chimney-piece in the entrance hall. The date recalls much
of the rebuilding following the fire in 1866.*

The staircase

His Lordship's room - the only room to be saved from the fire.

Didsbury, The Old Parsonage

In the days when Didsbury Wakes was the great festival of the many acred townships to the south of Manchester, the rush-cart was made where the rushes and the withies grew at Withington, and on St. Oswald's day was escorted by dancing and singing men, as if it were the ark of the Lord, to the old church at Didsbury. Then came a week of hospitality, feasting, and revelry – unbridled revelry. The church stood high above the marshlands of the Mersey, surrounded with black-and-white houses, common land, shooting-butts for archery, and the two inns so necessary in a large and straggling parish.

Everything is gone excepting some bits of the church, of the inns, and possibly of this house of which and in which I now write. The Wakes are nearly forgotten, the green is long since enclosed, the roads are narrowed, the last thatched farmstead has lately vanished. There are two inns, though the sign of "The Ring o' Bells" is gone. He who from the main road would go to church must pass between them, and therefore when what is sometimes called The Gospel is being preached, they are likened to 'The Gates of Hell' and lament is made that they are left to tempt the sinner from the path of duty to the church and the collection.

Over the stables of the Cock Inn, and extending into this house, is a large upper room called The Wakes Room, but why the inn and the parsonage should overlap and have bricked-up doorways, I, the owner, never could understand. There were more connections between Church authorities and alehouses when church-ales were common; amid our pilgrimages, [we have been] shown inns or hostels that were built and maintained out of abbey funds.

In the time of the Commonwealth there was an agreement made between the inhabitants of

the parish, or parochial (chapelrye, of Didisburye) and their minister, Mr. Thomas Clayton, from which I make the following extract:

'Item. That the mesuage and tenem[t] assigned to the use of the minister of the said church, for the tyme beinge, shall bee valued and acompted at the rate of tenne pounds p. ann. (towards the said xl £ p.ann.) considringe the tymes and that Mr. Clayton is a single man and soe cannot husband it to advantage.'

The above-mentioned house is probably the central part of this old parsonage. The rates alone are now many times the former rental; in fact, they would take all the poor man's £40 of income so let us consider the times and be sorry for the tenant and owner, who is still single and "soe cannot husband it to advantage.'

The ancient history of the place is lost because there are no very old deeds to any property in Didsbury. Even the Mosley family, who bought the manors of Manchester and Withington in about 1596, have none. The title to this place begins with an Act of Parliament of 1786 re the estates of the Bamfords of Bamford, who had inherited some (this being probably a part) from a John Davenport of Stockport. The Act cost William Bamford £550 and to raise that sum he sold for it 'All that ancient messuage or inn known by the sign of the Cock, with the barn and shippen thereunto belonging . . . with three other small antient messuages or dwelling-houses adjoining . . . orchards, garden, and vacant land,' to Sam Bethell, a joiner, to repair or erect better buildings and pay a small chief rent, which rent I now pay to the Countess of Dundonald, who inherited the Bamford-Hesketh estates. Bethell paid the £550 in 1795, and one Sam Newell, probably a lawyer, witnessed. The Cock Inn and adjoining shop would then be built, for the former "antient" buildings were timber framed and thatched. In 1804, Bethell sold out for £1,250, the buyer mortgaging for £1,000. The mortgage deed consists of five big skins of parchment, though the original deed of conveyance was only one smaller skin. A mortgage bond for £2,000 was also given, though he had only received £1,000, so we may conclude the poor man fell among lawyers, who stripped him, leaving him half dead. They also altered the spelling of 'antient shippen' to 'ancient shippon'.

Above: In the library

65

In 1832 the property was sold for £2,450, so it had doubled in value again, and up to the present time I find it has doubled with every generation. I have known many instances in our city and neighbourhood where the value of land has doubled with each generation; that is, it has gone up eightfold in the century.

In 1832 a Richard Fletcher of Birch Hall found £2,000, and a William Newall, a grocer, £450, for the purchase of this property. They sold to Louisa Titley, who made it over to trustees, for a marriage 'is intended to be had and solemised' between her and the Reverend Sam Newal, curate of Didsbury and in the occupation of the house. They were married, the young wife soon died, the flock gossiped, the parson left, but he or his kept the property though they sold the advowson of the living. As the house was haunted, and the new parson was always quarrelling with his landlord (the old one), a new rectory was built far away from the church about the time the old parish or parochial chapelry of Didsbury with its four rapidly increasing townships was joined ecclesiastically to Manchester. The patronage of the small and select bit of parish left with the old church was kept in private hands, and the cure of souls 'advertised'. Perhaps this open traffic in the curing of our souls has not been for the good or the peace of the shorn flock during the last two centuries. It was always likened to the curing of bacon, but nowadays few care and very few seem to know how to cure souls or bacon.

Parson Newall repaired the parsonage house and added the two higher rooms at the ends. He also planted the weeping ash on the lawn, in about 1840. The lime trees to the east were put in about 1830. Only a few of the old trees remain. Forest trees grew all round the garden, but I cut down one every winter, and at every fall the neighbours howled. There is a very old filbert close to the house that bears nuts every year, and very good ones they are. A Keswick apple also drops its fruit on to the lawn, for we never gather them, but eat them off the grass, if the birds or choir-boys leave any.

On 8th March 1865, we became tenants of the house. It had been empty for some time, the gardens were overgrown with fruit trees, and we were told it was very desirable to shut out the churchyard. As we had only flitted from the next house we brought many large evergreens with us, and elsewhere I have kept records of some of these trees and also of others planted in later years. The yews and the cedars of Lebanon are all measured. The apple trees are being choked by mistletoe, though it never grew in this district before I sowed its berries here. At the present time there are bamboos, palms, and camellias flourishing in the open air, for the house is on a bank of good gravel. Every room faces south-south-west, the warmest aspect it could have, as the sun shines straight in soon after one o'clock. It stands 125 feet above the level of the sea, in longitude 2. 15.30 west, and therefore its solar time is nearly ten minutes later than that of Greenwich.

As a haunted house the place was famous. There were shutters or iron bars to every window, but they did not keep out the ghosts. Servants would not stay when the bells were often rung at all hours and the nightly noises were incessant. The parsons should have laid the ghosts when they lived here, but they didn't; the ghosts abode, the parsons fled. We became used to them, possibly preferring them to the others. The wise mother told us they would not hurt us if we were good and quiet, but as a young man I have often jumped out of bed and rushed after something in the passages or on the stairs and caught – nothing, although that nothing could be plainly heard and seen.

'We meet them at the doorway, on the stair,
Along the passages they come and go,
Impalpable impressions on the air,
A sense of something moving to and fro.'

*This page and previous: Two more views of the library where
presumably Fletcher Moss wrote his many books*

The old staircase with stall-ends from Barlow

The name of Dieulacres Abbey is spelt all sorts of ways. I find four different spellings on one page of old records. The site is close to the town of Leek, where Hugh Cyveliok died. It seems probable to me that he may have been killed or had some accident when hunting that history has not recorded, for here his son transferred a colony of white monks from Pulton on the Dee. The monks were taken from the fury of the Welsh, but they may have looked back longingly on that pleasant land when they found themselves in those bleak, barren, wind-swept moors, where even the place-names reminded them of wolves, or boars, or stones.

Randle Blondevill (or white town, from the place of his birth), Earl of Chester, was a remarkable man, perhaps the most powerful man in England, a Prince of Wales, had five earldoms, two or three wives but no children, was a Crusader, did 'great atchievements', and wrote a book! He married a prince's widow, Constance in name. They were divorced and each married again, she dying of leprosy in a year, and he marrying another widow, when he ought to have been wary of any more. He locked the French king up in Lincoln Cathedral with his followers, and made him swear on the gospels on the altar that he would never lay claim to England, but hasten off out of the realm at once. Then he brought the youth Henry III from a cowshed and set him on the altar, and caused all the nobles to swear fealty to him. He was in the wars in France, and went on a crusade, where, on the return journey, a great storm arose, and when the ship was nearly lost he told the sailors that if they could only keep it going to midnight they would be all right and safe, for then his monks would

be praying for him. All which turned out as he prophesied, and the storm assuaged at once; at least the monks said so. Something that we may still see did come to pass from this crusade, for he built Beeston Castle, with its towers copied from Byzantium or Constantinople, and some of them remain to this day.

A new house seems to have arisen on the old one, for on the porch is the date 1612 and the initials of T. and A. B. The gateway has another date, of which 67 are the last figures. It is made of odd pieces of highly sculptured stone, a king and a saint being on either side. All over the farm buildings are bosses, saints heads, gargoyles, an Agnus Dei, and the end of a calf-cote has a very fine stone coffin lid engraved with cross and sword. Even the pigsties are partly made of the stones of the abbey. What became of the heart of the great earl, the founder, which was here buried? Perhaps the pigs ate it. Why should not they? It is a free country, and he would have eaten them. It is also said to be a Christian country, with a national church by law established, but queer things are done in it.

We went to have a look at the old church at Leek and, leaving our bikes by the churchyard rails, X was going into the church a little before me, when a sexton stopped him, saying they could not have cyclists in the church, so X naturally consigned the church to condemnation, and went off; but I persisted in going in, and found it what might have been expected. A church that has plainly once been fine and beautiful, with all the beauty restored away.

A coffin lid built into a barn

The current Abbey Farm

Part of the rear elevation

Our road onwards from Wybunbury becomes more undulating and beautiful. At the first gates of Doddington there lately stood a fine old black and white house, known as the Boar's Head, but it has been rebuilt in the fashion of the day. Further on are many picturesque cottages that tempted us to tarry on our way. An old woman begged us to photograph her cat. If the disreputable looking beast with its scratched face had been in my garden, I should have been willing to do something, but it went after the birds, and another, a quieter one, came and is shown in the picture [not reproduced in this compilation] sitting placidly under a gooseberry bush, though two women were cackling at it all the time.

We cycled about the park, photographed the Castle, and dawdled time away, hoping that some one would come to see what we were doing, and then we might ask questions; but nobody came, and the birds chattered at us, for the remnant of the Castle appears to be railed round and left for the birds. Its upper chambers, with their broken windows, should be an ideal home for owls. The cuckoo's call came from the neighbouring garden, where, perhaps, he was searching the gooseberry bushes for caterpillars, and slowly we walked across the park, skirting the wilder part where the red deer dwell, until we came to the London road.

Two views of the park gates

Remains of Doddington Castle

Dutton Hall, nr. Frodsham

There is here one of the most beautiful old halls that I ever saw spoilt – a magnificent carved oaken hall cut up into three storeys and little bedrooms. It must have been at one time like a small cathedral made of oak. Lofty, clustered columns, with a most beautiful roof in the attics, where the starlings build, and the lovely bosses of carved flowers and mouldings are gone. In the bedrooms you may read bits of deeply-cut inscriptions on the oaken cornice; then you have to go into the next room, and the next, and so on, to follow up the writing. A long account in wonderful carving and spelling commemorates the building of the house in 1539 'bi the especiall devising of Sr piers dutton… and after long sute before all the nobulls and jugs (judges) of this realme bi the space of vii yeres and above the same Sr piers was appioted heir malle… of all duttons land and so adjuged…' This is supplemented by the beautiful entrance, over which there is plainly inscribed, 'Syr Peyrs Dutton Knyght Lorde of Dutton and my lade dame julian hys wiff made this hall and buyldyng in ye yere of our Lorde God mcccccxlii [1542] who thanketh God of all.'

He certainly had need to thank God for all, though one would have thought that, considering he had gotten it by robbing the charities, the poor, the sick, and the church, the less said about it the better. For this was the same Sir Peter who went to hang the abbot of Norton, and it is evident his wealth and power came from the robbery of the religious houses, the great source from whence nearly every one of the proud families of Cheshire derive their wealth. He reminds me of one of the head-men in the Church and State party in Manchester, who told me that his chief reason for going to church was to pray that the horse he had backed might win its race.

Inside the outer doorway, which is filled now with slight modern work, is an enormously massive old oaken door, deeply carved, with the usual smaller door as part of it, evidently the great door of the abbey of Norton. Above and round it are large carved bosses, having sacred signs, the five wounds, a scapegoat, camel, bear, &c., and again, 'Who thakyth god of all xxxix.' Stupendous hinges, gorgeous coats-of-arms, carved columns and rare old work are there, the stolen spoils of the once great neighbouring abbey.

This grand house was probably 'warmed' at the marriage of the two daughters of Sir Piers Dutton on the feast of St. John the Baptist in 1542, when all the musicians and minstrels of Cheshire marched in procession before the happy couples. For the lords of Dutton had the licensing of the county minstrels from those far-off days when Randle, Earl of Chester, was in jeopardy by the wild Welshmen. Roger Lacy, surnamed Hell or Hellfire Roger from his fierce spirit, with his steward Dutton of Dutton, gathered all the rabble of Chester Midsummer Fair, males and females, fiddlers and tinkers, and rushed to the rescue. That was the Randle who bought all the land between the Ribble and the Mersey for forty marks of silver, the equivalent of about a hundred sacks of flour as nearly as I can reckon it.

As each sack of flour should make a hundred loaves of bread the reader may reckon for himself, and also remember that the value may go up in the future as much as it has gone up in the past.* Therefore, what may that bit of land be worth some day? The Earl of Chester, in gratitude for his deliverance, conferred on his rescuers the right to license all the gentlemen and ladies of easy virtue, learnedly styled "omnium leccatorium et meretricum,' in the county of Chester, to practise their vocations. In process of time it came to pass that musicians were not necessarily rogues, though they were so considered in Elizabeth's time, the exception being in Cheshire, where they were licensed as described below in the next century:

The author's father was a corn merchant.

'...all and every useinge and p'essinge ye noble art, ye worthy science and high misterie of musique and minstrellzie ... pub'cly here to drawe forthe their sundry instruments of musique and minstrellzie and to play heere pub'cly unto ye court house. This omitt you nott as you will at yo'r perills aboyde ye rebuke of ye Court, ye forfeiture of your instruments, and imprisonments of your bodyes. God save ye Kinges Maty, his most hon'ble counsell, and the Lord of Dutton, and send us peace. Amen.' Then they had to go to church and play 'a sett of lowd musique upon their knees,' singing 'God bless the King and the heir of Dutton.' Of course it all ended with a dinner just as if they were common councillors, and the music would no doubt be of a very miscellaneous character.

Porch of Dutton Hall

Fulleshurst Hall, (now Fullhurst), Nantwich

One day I was searching the map for somewhere about South Cheshire or North Shropshire, and found to my surprise the name of Fulleshurst Hall. Could it be the old home of the Fulleshursts, or Fowleshursts, who owned Crewe for generations and whose original habitat is not mentioned in history? I set off to find it on the first fine day, leaving the train at Nantwich, and without asking the way or going astray, being guided by the map only, I went right to it, and satisfied myself by the first glance that I had found the site of a very ancient home, the home of a family who had taken their name from it but had gone to a larger domain and there had died away.

The evidence of antiquity was the moat that half encircles the house now. Beyond the moat on one or two sides the ground slopes steeply to a brook, and it seemed to me the place may have had a decoy or been suitable for wildfowl before the farmland around was drained. Hence the name Fowleshurst, and the squire of that name who became famous at Poictiers. I have already retold the little that is known about him, and shown his effigy, with the name of his Captain engraven on his forehead, silently waiting for his Captain's call.

There were many delays before X could be induced to accompany me on another journey and photograph the place, and when we got there, the sight of "restorers" rebuilding and modernising the house nearly knocked me off the bicycle. The house I had seen a few months before was ages younger than the moat, but might be two hundred years old. It was having new windows, with pointing of bricks, the garden like a builder's yard, and everything in disorder. Only the moat remained, or rather the half of it, and for that I was thankful. It is picturesque. If a sanitary inspector saw it with the cows drinking at it he would be shocked, and he would want to serve a notice on the occupier to drain the premises, provide a fresh supply of clean water, level the yard, raise the roofs of the cowhouses, and pave them with cemented floors: costing more money than the place would be worth, and making it look like an ugly towyard.

Gawsworth Rectory and Hall

Arriving at the cottage by the church gates we found men working at fortifications round the churchyard, with notices saying no one could be admitted who had not previously received the sanction of the rector and churchwardens. As we had not had any notice of this notice it was impossible to comply, though I had no doubt the rector would admit us if he could be found. Therefore I went to the rectory, but found the garden gate locked, with a big notice on it: 'Private grounds. Trespassers will be prosecuted.'

I rang the bell three times, but there was no answer. I hesitated whether to keep on ringing, for there was evidently some one inside the house. A man who was working at the fortifications and was careful to lock the churchyard gate after him as he went in or out, sent a stable boy to me. From him I learnt that the rector was in the house, but 'when 'e's lock'd issel in 'e wunner come out.' I asked if there were no maid-servants to answer the bell, and the answer was, ''e wunner let 'em.' When I said something about the ordinary civilities or courtesies of life, the poor lad only seemed ashamed for his master, so the next thing we did was to rig up the camera in the road and photograph the rectory, taking care to focus for the notice on the gate.

Fortunately the best positions for photographing Gawsworth Church and hall are on the road, where every detail of them may be seen reflected in the clear water of the pools. Only two of these ancient fish ponds are left. The sites of others may be seen, for the fish-eating Churchmen of old

The offending Rectory!

80

had many ponds, not only for variety, but that some might be run dry and ploughed up to breed finer fish. The woman at the cottage told us she had notice to quit after living there for nearly twenty years, rearing a family and eking out a living by showing the church. X had set up his camera and was about to take the cap off when some one frightened the wild-ducks on the pool, and all the reflections in the water were destroyed. A little patience set that right. Again all was ready, when some dense smoke rolled over everything, quite stopping photography. The smoke evidently came from a rubbish heap in the rectory garden, and X, who was very religiously brought up, burst out, saying it was that something parson doing it on purpose. He had been thinking of the words another parson lately used when speaking of the Sultan, but I was alarmed that his placid temper should be so ruffled, and suggested we sang a hymn, something about

'Where every prospect pleases,
And only man is vile.'

Time and patience brought satisfactory exposures, and we sat by the waterside, eating apples and talking politics. There is a beautiful church that was once by force stolen from the Roman Catholics. It is now kept locked up at the caprice of one man, who, according to Crockford, receives more than £1 per annum per head of the population of the parish. One of the ancient inscriptions in it was 'Orate pro aia Georgii Baguley rectoris hujus ecclesiae qui rectoriam de novo construxit' (Pray for the soul of George Baguley, rector of this church, who built the rectory anew). Other times bring other manners; other prayers are now wanted, and one more restitution, and that is the church to be free and open to all.

Gawsworth Hall

Gawsworth Church, where entry was denied to Fletcher Moss

Handforth Hall

The earliest records of the place are romantic tales of the Honfords of Honford, who seem to have been a rough-and-ready breed, only at peace when they were fighting, and not very particular as to marriage or murder. At least one of them was a Crusader, for when in the Holy Land a star fell from heaven in front of the armies of Saladin, Honford of Honford instantly seized it, and, fixing it to his shield, it became the cognizance of his race. If any Thomas-a-Didymus doubt, he may see the star in the glass of the Honford chapel in Cheadle church, where it has borne its silent testimony for more than three hundred years.

Another of the family was a witness of the mystery and tragedy of Joan of Arc: and when the fiery cross went round the Scots for the invasion of England, and every manor or parish in Lancashire and Cheshire sent its best manhood to meet them, the last Honford of Honford, the last heir-male of his race, fell with so many of his neighbours and kinsfolk on the famous Cheviot moor.

Sir Edward Stanley, immortalised in *Marmion* was Lord of Bosley near Macclesfield. Christopher Savage, the mayor of Macclesfield, and so many of the townsmen fell in the fight that for some years afterwards a quorum of substantial burgesses could not be formed to govern the town. Randle Bebington of Bebington, with William, Handle, James, John and Charles, the sons of his brother, were all killed. Venables, the twenty-first lord of Kynderton, Sherd of Disley, Maisterson of Nantwich, Fouleshurst of Crewe, with many more of the local squires and gentry, were dead upon the field. The Abbot of Vale Royal went with three hundred of his tenantry, and perhaps every name in Cheshire was represented, for we may read of Fittons, Duttons, Dones and others. These are they who won the victory. A Scotsman has written of the other side –

'Tradition, legend, time, and song,
Shall many an age that wail prolong
Still from the sire the son shall hear
Of the stern strife and carnage drear
On Flodden's fatal field:
Where shiver'd was fair Scotland's spear
And broken was her shield.'

Though the last male Honford had fallen, the romance of the race survived, for the dead squire had left a little daughter. She was at once married to Sir John Stanley, a son of the Bishop of Ely, who 'lived with one who was not his sister, and who wanted nothing to make her his wife save marriage.' The united ages of the newly-wedded couple would not be quite thirty. She was about ten, and heiress to the estates of the Honfords. He had nought to inherit, but his natural father looked after him, and, as our oldest glee says, 'Merrily sang the monks of Ely,' so Ely's bishop got his son wed to the heiress, and a notable man he proved. He was seventeen when he led four thousand men into the battle, and an old ballad says: 'There never was bairn born That day bare him better'

Sir Walter Scott's version says:
'Let Stanley charge with spur of fire
With Chester charge and Lancashire,
Full upon Scotland's central host,

Or Victory and England's lost.'

After the Cheshire bowmen did their fell work, the charge won Flodden for England. Dim traditions tell of churchyard yews still living that furnished bows for Flodden. Speke Hall still shows its trophies. Manuscript records of witnesses exist, and every parish around me sent men to that death-grip struggle on Flodden.

The new lord of Honford, or Handford or Handforthe as it was then variously spelt, was not suffered to be long in peace. His neighbour, Legh of Adlington, had married Joan Lark, a cast-off mistress of Cardinal Wolsey, and a quarrel arose between him and Sir John Stanley. The Leghs invoked the aid of the all-powerful cardinal, who had Stanley imprisoned, and it may be this Joan was the woman referred to by Shakespeare:

'I'll startle you
Worse than the sacrum bell, when the brown wench
Lay kissing in your arms, Lord Cardinal.'

Sir John was probably unjustly condemned, for it seems to have broken his heart. As far as he could, he settled his affairs, past, present, and future. In memory of his father, and for prayers for his parents, he built the Stanley chapel, in the cathedral of Manchester, and, in the inscription on its portal, dated it with the date of the battle, as may still be seen. From the Abbot of Westminster he bought 'letters of paternity' for himself, wife, and son, gave to trustees all he had, renounced his wife and all the pomps, vanities, pleasures and delectations of this world, avowed chastity, and became a Benedictine.

In the sacristy of St. Paul's, London, on the 25th June, 1528, 'in the face of the church', the married couple were solemnly divorced (or released), and he passes from our ken. His arms may still be seen in the churches of Cheadle and Manchester, always encircled by the mournful motto on Vanity and as I have written before – lands and funds he had already given for pious uses, penny doles to poor widows and poor maidens, wages to priests or poor who would pray for him, with many elaborate safeguards and quaint old terms long since forgotten, for all has passed into oblivion, and in our time who fingers the money or who does the praying no man knoweth.

The wife was to have entered into 'religion' also, but she thought better of it, and married again. Her second husband was Uryan, the ninth son of Sir Handle Brereton, and he built the hall of Handforth, as the inscription on the oaken portal shows today:

'This haulle was buylded In the yeare of oure Lord God m.ccccc.lxii by Uryan Breretoun Knight Whom maryed Margaret and heyre of Wyllyam Handforth of Handforthe Esquire and had Issue vi sonnes and ii daughters.'

This porch and inscription (with necessary differences) were copied in the new hall built for the neighbouring manor of Adlington by Thomas Legh when be married Sibbel, or Sybyl, a daughter of Uryan and Margaret. Another daughter of Uryan by his second wife, Alice Trafford, was Mary, the mother of Edward Barlow, the martyr. A brother of the Breretons was mixed up in the little scandal about Queen Anne Boleyn, and Sir William, the great-grandson of Uryan, was the commander-in-chief of the armies of Parliament for Cheshire and adjacent counties. He must have been extraordinarily active, for he fought battles and sieges in every town of the district. In days of peace he travelled abroad and at home, writing a diary of his journeys which is still interesting reading. He had men over from Holland to make a decoy for wildfowl. The site of it may be traced to-day down a winding stream opposite the hall to a small reservoir now used by calico printers.

Handforth Hall actually figures again in our last bit of civil war: the gallant but ill-starred attempt of Prince Charlie to win again the throne of his ancestors from the German George in the '45. The Prince left Manchester by the London road, turned at Rushford, and by Burnage Lane reached Didsbury, where be built the first bridge across the Mersey and got to Cheadle. Stockport was avoided because the bridge there was broken down and opposition threatened. From Cheadle to Macclesfield the route would be by Handforth Hall, and there the Prince rested and dined.

Two views of the Hall showing the entrance frontage

The Porch

The ornate staircase

Hawthorne Hall, Wilmslow

At Wilmslow we turn aside to photograph Hawthorne or Harethorne Hall, now being hemmed in by the builders on all sides. On a heap of builders' refuse the camera was set up, and over the garden fence X took a good picture of the many-gabled quaint house that was rebuilt within its pleasant park and gardens just two hundred years ago.

Hyde Hall, nr. Denton

Turning through a plain gateway, and crossing open fields or park under the stately remnants of an avenue, we approach the venerable and beautiful pile of Moreton Old Hall. It is probably the most picturesque of any of the timber-framed houses in the country, the most picturesque houses in the world. It is not kept up as the home of the wealthy, as are the lovely halls of Speke or Pitchford, for it is used as a farmhouse but still it is well kept. I should think it would take nearly all the rent of the farm to maintain the fabric in good repair.

The moat is square and broad, about eighty yards, or ten Cheshire rods, to the side, and the water is fairly clear. It is crossed by a stone bridge, immediately behind which rises the magnificent gatehouse. It is three storeys in height and backed by many quaint and curious old-fashioned rooms, time - worn enough, but probably not as old as the great hall or the glorious windows across the courtyard, the famous octagonal bays of Moreton. This quadrangular, pebbled courtyard, surrounded by a bewildering maze of cornered windows, dim recesses, infinite inscriptions, doorways, stairways, carved sentries, ornamental details, horse-block beyond the fortified entrance by the double door, all as it was three hundred years ago. It must be unique.

In giving a very slight and feeble description of this old home, I might begin with the words of our nurse and say: 'There's so much to be done I don't know where to turn me.' Most people begin with the inscriptions over the main windows, and quote them wrongly. As parts of them cannot be seen in the photographs, though most of them can, I will try to give them correctly, putting in brackets a bare mention of animals, which may be merely for ornament, or may have some reference to armorial bearings: 'God is al in al thing. This (fox) windous (hare) whire (man's head) made by William (dragon) Moreton in the yeare of (bear's head, the Brereton crest) oure Lorde MDLIX (bull's head, Bulkeley crest).'

Those are around the upper storey of the highly ornamented windows of the great 'Rycharde Dale Carpeder made thies windous by the Grac of God.' The letters are all capitals, the timber all oak, and most profusely carved at every cornice, gable, barge-board or pendant.

If we call this great hall and drawing-room the state apartments they face the south and the back of the fortified entrance under the grand gatehouse the front of which also faces the south. The four sides of the buildings are about square with the points of the compass. At the west side is the old kitchen with its original furniture, pewter with the Moreton crest, and a spice chest with drawers enough to hold all the spices of Araby the Blest and all the herbs our grandmothers ever knew. On the east of the quadrangle is the chapel, perhaps the oldest bit of the place. Churches and public-houses do endure longer than most buildings.

This one is rather remarkable for the chancel and the nave (if I may use the customary terms) are so tiny, being only a few yards square, and the nave is without a window, having the priest's room over it. A rood screen goes up to the ceiling, but through it may be seen on the chancel walls very old texts in black letter which are almost illegible. At the east end is a plain pointed window of five lights. It is evident that very few sinners were expected or intended to worship here in the good old days, although there was once a bishop in the family. In the well-known *Itinerary of Vale Royal* we may read that this place:

'gave breeding to that famous Bishop Moreton, which in the time of Richard the Third, the usurper, contrived that project of the marriage of the two heirs of the houses of York and Lancaster, from whence proceeded the happiness that we enjoy at this day.'

This refers to Shakespeare's John Morton, Bishop of Ely, whom Richard addressed in the well-known words in the vivid scene of the withered arm and the accusation of Hastings:

'My lord of Ely, when I was last in Holborn,
I saw good strawberries in your garden there;
I do beseech you send for some of them.
Marry, and will, my lord with all my heart.'

Here is another bit of history, this time out of Ormerod, who has struggled hard to make an authentic pedigree. It refers to the father of the builder of the hall, who was evidently a keen one, and perhaps the first 'which should sit highest in the churche and foremost goo in procession.' They left the case to the Justice Bromley and Sir William Brereton, and, doubtless after spending freely in law and folly, they received an award which might lead them to further litigation 'He that may dispende in landes by title of enheritaunce ten mark or above more than the other.' So the judge and the knight and 'twelve of the most auncyent men in Astebery' thought little of the blue blood and the prodigious pedigrees of their squabbling squires, but reckoned them up as if they were mere property jobbers. In after years their children, Tom Rode and Alice Moreton, married and patched up the quarrel that way. Their granddaughter, Alice, married a neighbour, John Lowndes of Overton, from whom in eighth descent came our friend X. [Fletcher Moss's photographer James watts who lived at Abney Hall.]

Let us spend our day exploring nooks and corners of this fine old rambling building. There are four circular staircases, winding up and down to endless empty rooms, entering from one another, wonderfully adapted for hide-and-seek or ghosts, or nightly noises, for they are beautifully panelled in grand old oak. The designers had great care for sanitary matters, as there are several closets, like little rooms, projecting from the outer walls, with chimney flues turned upside down. The modern cheese-room was formerly two secret chambers, access to which was by a cunningly hidden sliding panel near to the floor, with a hole for retreat which may have led under the moat, but probably gave access to the garden only. There seem to have been several little doors from the house to the garden ready for emergencies.

The newel post, round which the stairs wind to the ballroom over the gatehouse, is one straight oak to the top of the three storeys. The doors from the stairs to the rooms all have primitive fastenings, with great bars of oak to bolt right across them into holes in the wall.

The ballroom itself is a most beautiful old room. Long and narrow, just the thing for the old-fashioned country dances, it is panelled with splendidly grained oak to about four feet high, and above that is nearly all windows with richly patterned leadlights, through which the sun or the moon may cast fantastic shadows on the rocky floor or oaken walls. The floors are of cement, which time has caused to roll up and down in undulations that are amusing to the walker, but might be troublous to the dancer. The ceiling is diapered with timber in pattern and the ends of the room have figures and mottoes. A blindfolded figure of Fortune with a wheel over her head has 'The wheele of Fortune whose rule is ignoraunce,' the wheel bearing 'Qui modo scandit corruet statim,' which may be translated, 'Who climbs at all may tumble any time.' At the other end of the room a figure of Destiny or Fate transfixing a globe has 'The speare of destinye whose ruler is knowledge.'

There are other writings on the glass and on the walls, for the vulgar, modern cad has even cut his repulsive initials into the finely grained oak, and English oak with such medullary markings could not now be gotten for love or money. Some of the old writings are worth copying. though the originals cannot be found. An old Tory writes 'All change I scorne. Men can noe more know women's mind by Kaire than by her shadow judge what clothes shee weare...'

A view from the drive

*Top: The house from the Moat. Bottom: The fantastic detail
which helps to make the house so endearing*

The gatehouse from the courtyard

The Porch

Richard Dale's window

A small room over the entrance

The Ballroom

Mees Hall, west of Stone, Staffordshire

As this pilgrimage was mainly to the place from whence came the direct male line of my fathers, and must therefore relate to family history more than some readers would like, this timely notice will enable them to skip it before they are wearied.

The etymology and derivation of names is an interesting study, especially when it is one's own name that is under investigation, and the changes that time has wrought in it as in all other things are known. When under the inquisition of the catechism we are asked what is our name and who gave us that name, it is all very well to put the responsibility of it on to our god-parents, but where did *they* get it from? Now, my Christian name Fletcher was a surname meaning a fledger, or featherer of arrows, and Moss was almost certainly given as a distinguishing name to some male ancestor who lived on or by a moss.

It happened that my father was born at a very old house known as Mees Hall, which still stands near to the railway a little past Standon Bridge station, on the left as one goes from Crewe to Stafford. It is built of big blocks of warm-coloured stone up to the eaves, with stone mullioned windows, three timber-built gables, and big stone chimneys, and it stands by the little river Mees or Sow. The family left the place in the severe depression that came on the yeomen of England after the long wars with Napoleon, my grandfather selling his last bit of land in 1816. The hall, which was very old then, is now owned by the Fitzherberts of Swynnerton, and looks as if precious little had been spent on it in the last hundred years.

The name of Mees, though very short, is spelt in different ways even on the signposts in the road. There are Coldmeese and Millmeece. Long ago I had wondered if Mees and Moss had originally been the same name, and lately I looked for the place in the great book which is the foundation of all local history, the Domesday Survey of the Conqueror. There I found 'In Mess Vlfere tenuit Tra e II car,' which I translate In Mess Wolfer held two carucates of land.' Another entry says 'In Ecleshelle Ipse eps ten in Mess' – 'In Eccleshall the bishop himself holds Mess'. Therefore the Church, in the shape of the bishops of Chester, grabbed the Saxon's land, and I have somewhere read that in after years the Priory of Ronton, a neighbouring religious house under the abbey of Haughmond, claimed some rights.

The Anglo-Saxon dictionary gives 'meos' as their word for moss, the spelling looking like a compromise between moss and mess and to make a note by the way, let me say that Ulf, or some compound of the word, were common names with the Saxons when wolves were common in the land. In 1086 Wolfer held Mess. In 1812, Eliza Moss was born at Mees Hall, married a Woolf, and is still living within a mile of the place in full possession of her faculties, able to eat, drink, sing, and be merry at the age of ninety years.

To continue my search I looked up the Court Rolls for Staffordshire, and soon found many variations of the name, for to get into trouble and debt seems characteristic of the family. At the Stafford Assize of 1278 there is a notable entry, for it gives both forms of spelling the same short name – 'Matilda, the widow of William del Mos, sued Richard, the son of William del Mes, for a third of a messuage and two virgates of land in Eddishale as her dower. Richard stated that he held as heir to his mother Margaret, and William, his father, never held the tenement in fee but only by courtesy of England, and therefore could not endow.' This was about the time when surnames were coming into use, and it is evident that some William of Mos or Mes was taking his name from his land, which is still in the parish of Eccleshall, and that he had been married twice. In 1361 William del Mosse senior had his wife stolen, and actually made a fuss about it at the Stafford Assize.

Other generations come, and another William del Mosse was parson of Langport and one of the founders of the college of Tong. Another century and more rolled away, and in 1539 it was feared the Pope would invade England to avenge the robbery of his Church, when another William Mosse turned up as 'a bilman without horse or harness.' Then parish registers were instituted, and the neighbouring parishes of Eccleshall, Standon, and Swynnerton have plenty of material for the enterprising pedigree hunter, the difficulty being to disentangle the entries.

May I insert here a curious old family legend which is absolutely true? It is that if any child of our family be christened Anne or a similar name it will very soon be dead. My father had twelve brothers and sisters, only one of whom, namely Anne, died in infancy. With the preceding generations the fatality had always been the same, and when our time came my mother, whose mother had trained her in the customs of the Quakers, would call her first daughter Hannah, after her favourite sister. My father's family foretold disaster, at which my mother only smiled, but the child soon died, and she did not try the name again. In the Standon registers, as far back as 1594, I found the entry of baptism of Anne, the daughter of John and Anne Moss, but that child was soon buried though all the others were reared.

When my father was christened (which was safely performed at Standon) some of the guests who were bidden to the feast became what they termed 'market-fresh' and one who enthusiastically kept up old customs even to 'Tummusing' on St. Thomas's day, was, when riding home through the little river 'misbespilt' off the

pillion into the water, where she peacefully sat 'quite humble and calm.'

This page and opposite: Mees Hall

Moss Hall, Audlem

We went by the usual train to Crewe, and from thence to Audlem, to photograph the many-gabled black and white house known as Moss Hall. The date that is now over the door is 1016, but the second figure has probably been a six, and the person who altered it deserved kicking. In the Civil War time a Captain Massy (not Mossy) lived here, and was plundered of sixty cattle with goods and horses all at once. How he would swear! Church and King men to this day are great in oaths, and some of them would not be within adding a few centuries to the date of the house or the long descent of the family. Even if this Massy were a Puritan, and I rather think he was on the side of the Parliament, he might be excused a little strong language at losing his cattle and having to seek consolation and revenge from the Old Testament's denunciations of the wicked and the sinner.

Audlem village has a little quaint old church perched up on a steep bit of rock in its midst. Like other open churches it is well kept, has been fairly well restored without being spoilt, and has several interesting bits of architecture, old heads, old oak, and marks in the ancient porch that may have been caused (as the legends say) by the sharpening of arrow heads. There is a disused doorway high up which looks as if any one stepped out of it now he would step into empty space. Then there is a butter market at the bottom of the church steps, but there is no butter, no women, and no one about. Every one seems asleep even at noon. A calm and placid little town where the kittening of a cat would cause some temporary excitement.

Muckleston Wood, Staffordshire
(South of Woore)

We soon begin to mount again. Stonier and steeper becomes the lane until at last we reach the gate to Mucklestone Wood. Stretching ourselves amid the gorse, broom and bracken we breathe that glorious air and almost gasp at the great scene that is spread out before us. No picture could be painted to do justice to that. The landscape is too vast, the details too crowded. The house itself stands plain and lonely, a well-known landmark when at varying intervals it gets a coat of white-wash. It was built in 1777, far from other houses, partly as a home for for an idiot, and has been through many changes. The drawing is from a water colour that I took forty years ago [1863]. The two birch trees joined together like the Siamese twins was a favourite seat of mine.

Norman Hall

On one of Cheshire's pleasant hills there is a timeworn house with a grand name but no history – not a scrap of history, legend, or tale that I can learn, and yet its name with its beautiful country should bring wealth for a magnificent restoration, if it were only known to some of our neighbours on whom new riches have rolled.

Norman Hall – what an attraction to an enterprising member of the great families of Smith, or Jones, or Brown, or Robinson, who can read and write and has made tons of money (it not being necessary that he should speak English), and who sighs for the old house at home where his forefathers dwelt. He finds it here, dismantled, derelict and desolate, but ready to revive under his genius and his gold. More than once has plain Mr. Smith assumed a Norman name and appropriated ancestors as much akin to him as was Mr. Tubal-Cain who was fond of brass on the east side of the garden of Eden. He has even got barristers, 'gentlemen learned in the law,' who ought to have been above selling themselves, to edit and endorse his fudge. Here might be the long-lost home of a romantic race!

For ages, Cheshire's knights and esquires with their serfs and vassals served under their Earls, the Kings of England, in their wars beyond the sea – singing with the troubadours 'Our King is gone to Normandy' and some battered, war-worn warrior, whose luck had brought him home again, may have built this 'Norman Hall' on the land where he was born. Now he is 'gone hence.' There is no record of his life or death. There is no legend or tale. The heirs and the mourners are gone. The sighs have ceased. The very name and memory are all forgotten.

Another view of the house, Norman Hall

Oversley

A little past the steep descent to Oversley Ford, we turn down a very narrow rough road to the right, where stands a cottage, thatched and tumbledown, of varied heights and age. It was shut up, with no one near. A very ancient yew grows by its side. Masses of ivy enshroud a dormer window and picturesque gable. The damson trees around are white as snow, but the light is against us, and I particularly want a photograph, having reason to believe that from this very house my mother's mother's mother, whose name was Betty Roylance, was married to James Barratt at Wilmslow, in 1771. The house this James Barratt, my mother's grandfather, built at Hale Barns is not far off, but is not very picturesque. When playing as a child in the garden there she was frightened by a snake; a fascinating snake-tale for her children.

For us, as common pilgrims of the day, let us sit about the tombs and learn what they tell us. Firstly, any one accustomed to church-yards would soon note the great quantity of gravestones with quaint and beautiful letter-ing, and sixteen hundred odd for date. These are rare anywhere, and very much rarer is a flag or stone of the previous century. We find one of 1599 where the five is like the letter S, a very old-fashioned form. Here is the name of a man who left some money to the parish, Ouffe. The modern slang for money is 'ouf.' It is proudly inscribed above Paul Ashton that he was father and grandfather to ninety-four children, and was aged ninety-five. The number of children were evidently gaining on the number of his years as he got older, for he must have had a good start. At Cheadle churchyard old Randy Allcock hon-estly confessed that he did not know how many children he left. No wonder the Allcocks and Ashtons are numerous in the district.

A great tomb with a long inscription tells how much money was raised for the widow and children of a quarryman named William Wyatt, who was shot dead, and whose brother was wounded by two highwaymen named Walmsley and Bate, who had tried to rob a man named Ernill. All happens in good order, for the robbers got hanged at last, and the epitaph ends, 'As for man his days are as grass, as a flower of the field so he flourisheth; for the wind passeth over it and it is gone, and the place thereof shall know it no more.'

Another nice little story of a freebooter is given in very original verse, which I copied most carefully; the last two lines rhyme exactly when spoken by the vulgar tongue:

'Beneath this stone lyes Edw'd. Green
Who for cutting stone famous was seen,
But he was sent to apprehend
One Joseph Clark, of Kerridge End,
For stealing deer of Esquire Downs,
Where he was shott and dyd o' th' wounds.'

The Old Vicarage, Prestbury

The Riddings, or Riddings Hall, Altrincham

Another timeworn home, around whose mouldering walls stagnates a shiny moat, lies to the west of mine. Britons may have named it from their word for ford being *rhyd*, or Anglo-Saxons from their ridding up the forest primeval. The earliest lords we know show in their names their Norman descent; Vawdreys and Gerards are not uncommon names in Cheshire history. But who cares for history now? Shrieking trains whiz close past the once-fortified home whose glories have departed. Suburban villas, semi-detached and semi-genteel, spring up like toadstools along its dirty lane. The newfangled folk from them say the water round the house must be unhealthy – the farmer says it's good enough to wash the 'taties and the onions for them to buy.

We retrace our way up the lane, go for a mile or two towards Mobberley, and turn across the fields to the left to a curious old house standing on the edge of Lindow Moss. It is named Saltersley, as if some of the brine-pits that were not uncommon in Cheshire had once been here. It seems strange for a solid stone house to have been built away from everywhere, with nothing but spongy moss in front and by its sides. It is low and solid, without date, but there is a long old-fashioned table within it that is dated 1639, so the house must have been built before then, or built round the table. Certainly the table cannot be got out of the house without pulling some of the walls down, or it would have been sold, for it is valuable. It is of massive oak, with six legs, and behind it is a Jacobean screen with raised seat, all redolent of faded gentility. From the initials, 'F. H.,' that are on the table, it was probably made for the Hulmes, who sold the small estate to the Strettels in 1662. Since then there have been many owners, and apparently poverty-stricken tenants, for the place has a weird, lost look. Begirt about as it is by quaking bog, it may some day go down quick into the pit, leaving only corpse-lights to flicker o'er the moss where once had been a human home.

Table and Screen at Saltersley

Sandbach

The celebrated crosses of Sandbach were the goal of many a genuine pilgrimage for centuries. Although they have been broken into bits and the bits have been carted away for miles, built into buildings, burned, and used for paving stones, they have been coming together again bit to bit after all their ill-treatment and wanderings. Now the battered crosses stand again in the marketplace above the din and the squalor of the market, and here are pictures of what remains of them after twelve hundred years of wear and tear.

It is said they were erected to commemorate the first preaching of Christianity in the kingdom of Mercia, and they were probably thrown down at the time of the great Civil War. Sir John Crewe of Utkinton set up the main part of the larger cross on his estate, carefully covering the crucified Christ with mortar, as he considered it to be a badge of popery, and his dread of popery was greater than his reverence for his Christ. From there this fragment went to Tarporley Rectory, and from thence to Oulton Hall. The lower part of the great cross had been built into the town well in Sandbach, and the end of the pillar was in a garden rockery. The top of the smaller cross was used as a step to a house, and other parts were made into pavement. The bits were pieced with other bits, and a brass records the 'liberality' of a man, who stole the greater part, in restoring the fragments.

The crosses stand on the old platform, and the old figures at the angles of the steps are still there, though they are worn away to almost shapeless stumps by the dirty children who seem to be always idly rubbing against them. The present height of the greater cross is given as sixteen feet eight inches, and of the lesser twelve feet. They have had circular heads, and the height of the larger from the ground has been estimated to have been originally from twenty-four to twenty-five feet. It undoubtedly commemorates scenes in the life of Christ, while the smaller cross is thought to record the first local preachers of Christianity.

Our photograph of the east side shows three figures in a circle, the outer ones apparently doing obeisance to the middle one. Above that are three figures, the one to the right having a dove above, the one to the left being probably Peter with the Keys. Higher again is a very plain representation of the Nativity, with the animals looking at the manger, and above that the crucified Christ with the four evangelists and

their emblems at the four corners. Still higher is a figure with head downwards and others indistinct and mutilated.

The northern side shows eleven apostles being breathed on by a flying monster having a terrible triple cloven tongue. The heads of the crosses are thought to have been circular, pierced with figures as spokes in a wheel.

The church has been so thoroughly restored by Sir Gilbert Scott, I had better say nothing about it; the spire has gone altogether. The old registers remain, and one entry seems to me to be worth copying. It is as follows:

'1598. Baptized Williams Leversage son of William
Leversage gentleman was baptized the fifth day of
June; William Leversage, William Bulkeley, Esquires,
William Yardley, William Lawton, William Moreton,
William Smethwicke, William Allen, William Hassall,
William Llandyn and Elizabeth Delves being the godparents and sponsors of the said child.'

There are many ale-houses in the little town, where anyone who has a penny may sample the 'dagger stuff,' and some of these old inns are very picturesque, for licensed houses last much longer than ordinary houses, though their tenants have much shorter lives than similar folk in other occupations.

The Bear is dated 1634 with the initials R. K. The old Hall is dated 1656 with the initials T. B. I cannot find any history of this old house or its original owners. It is doubtless on the site of the

first fortress or manor-house, for it is near to the church, and on a steep bank above a brook that appears to have nearly surrounded it. It occurred to me the parish registers might show who T. B. was, and he was probably the schoolmaster Thomas Baily, who died in the year of the building of the Hall. Folklore tells us that men who build grand houses generally die as soon as it is finished; and the schoolmasters of Sandbach had very unusual help from lands devoted to education.

At the top of the stairs in the old Hall there remains a good specimen of a dog-gate, with primitive paling across the landing so that dogs lame or sharp, two-legged or four-legged, might be debarred from getting into the bedrooms.

Previous page: The east side of the two crosses with what Fletcher Moss described as "dirty children"
Right: Another view of the restored crosses

115

The Old Hall Inn

The Old Hall Inn with the Dog gate (below)

The Bear Inn dated 1634, Sandbach

Siddington Church and its cross

Siddington Church

Slade Hall, Didsbury

Slade Hall is an old home on the north-east border of Didsbury, that has descended from father to son for ten generations.

A Richard Syddall, Siddall, or Sudal, a yeoman of Withington, appears to have prospered, and by his will in 1558 left the lease of his dwelling, Mylkewaleslade to his son Edward, on condition that he, without 'coneng craft or gile,' surrendered his 'meas'e and ten't [messuage and tenement] in Diddesburye' to Elizabeth his wife.

His 'shope in M'Keth strete, Manchester,' in default of Edward's heirs, went to his second son Tom.

In 1584 Edward bought Milkwall-Slade with 24 acres of land, garden and orchards, for £10 from Rauff and Joan Slade of Brerehurst, doing fealty to the lord of the manor. He rebuilt the house, his initials in a pretty little border, and the date 1585 in another, being now over the door. His son George apparently put his mark on also, for the initials G. S. are roughly cut out of the oaken lintel. The entry of the wedding of George Siddall to Margaret Fletcher, 1575, is still in the Didsbury registers. They shortened the name of the place to Slade, and the natives pronounce it Slate.

In 1664 Syddall was summoned to give an account of his arms and crest, but he seems not to have wanted any, probably thinking he could make better use of the money. Quietly and unostentatiously the years and the generations slipped away, son succeeding father, begetting children, and being gathered to his fathers. In their humdrum lives there seems little to record. They had the tenacity to stick to their home, and that is why they are here. Now the old home is gone from, them, not voluntarily but by compulsion, for the London and North-Western Railway Co., after cutting off some of the land has annexed the house. The oaken seats in the deep porch are daubed with paint, and over them is a dado stencilled in the latest fashion of railway station waiting-rooms. The fine old door with its hinges and handles is still intact. Let us hope it will escape improvements for an inquiry office. One of the upper rooms has very elaborate plaster work. There are the royal arms of Elizabeth, the arms of the Stanleys, Earls of Derby, and possibly those of Alderley, stag-hunts, figures, &c.

In the pursuit of knowledge, I had the temerity to ask the present Mr. Siddall, senr., what the estate realised, for with such a long record the history of its inevitable rise in value would be very interesting. More than thirty years ago I learnt, and have since often proved, that the value of land doubles with every generation. That is the rule, though of course there are exceptions to all rules, and cycles of good and bad years at all times. Taking three generations to the century, the value of land should increase eightfold in a hundred years. Let us sum up Slade.

1585 – £10 is the price of the estate of 24 acres, with an old house. In those days a good house, or part of a church, could be built for £5, but it will be better to ignore the house, for it is only a very old one to-day, and it is the value of the land that I am writing about.

1685 – £80 for the 24 acres would be about the value. Prices would be improving after the Civil War, when land was unsaleable.

1785 – £640, or £26 an acre. A fair value for land in the district. The Napoleonic wars were to bring a great rise, and corresponding decline.

1885 – £5,120 or £313 an acre. Are we getting lost in Geometrical Progression? The neighbouring city is rapidly advancing. Sites are being sought for building on, the days of farming are done, and the value is much greater than here stated.

1905. It has all gone, and although not one generation has passed since our last valuation, the

The entrance front

price has doubled again and again. In ten generations the original £10 has grown into more than £20,000. There were no rates in the old time – now they are always advancing, and we are told no one can live for them. Nine-tenths of our politicians and our infallible Press (a capital P this time, please) are constantly preaching and teaching of the ruin of the country from the rural population flocking into the towns. Here, the town's locusts have swarmed on to the country, and in the once pleasant gardens and orchards of Slade every green leaf is withering. There will not be one blade of grass left, for the desolating trail of the railway and the soulless builder of vulgar villadom have brought their blight on all.

Though the elder line of the Syddals lived uneventful lives, their kinsmen in Manchester made history, scrupling not to offer their lives as martyrs for their king and country.

The wills of the two earliest of the family mention a shop in Market Street or Market Place that, in case of some default, was to go to their younger son Thomas. The value of the shop or burgage was given as sixpence a year, and that would stand multiplying many times when we consider that some of the shops there now are worth £1000 a year. In 1690 a 'Pole' of Manchester records Thomas Siddall, wife and son, living in one of the first houses in Market Sted Lane, and therefore by the market-place.

At the death of Queen Anne in 1714, political and religious strife was at fever heat. Were the Stuarts to reign, and the risk to be run of the country slipping into Roman Catholicism or should a king be imported from Germany, and dismal dissent to have the upper hand? In Manchester there were riots, and a mob pulled down the Presbyterian chapel (now the Unitarian chapel in Cross Street) under the leadership of Tom Syddall. For that he was put in the pillory, and then in the prison at Lancaster.

The Stuart army, marching south, released all prisoners, and he joined it, only to be defeated at Preston and imprisoned again. Then came Lancaster's 'Bloody Assize' and thirty-four were hanged, drawn, and quartered. Five of them were done at Knot Mill, at a cost of £8.10s and Syddall's head was stuck up in the market-place by his own shop door.

There his son Tom daily saw it, and doubtless vowed, in his boy's way, to be avenged if ever the opportunity came. Thirty years after, he thought it came, and hesitated not to fling himself heart and soul into raising a regiment in Manchester, to help Prince Charles Edward in his gallant attempt to win again the crown of his ancestors. The ill-fated regiment surrendered as prisoners of war at Carlisle, on the written promise that they 'should not be put to the sword, but reserved for the king's pleasure.'

The pleasure of the German king, who was living with his German harlots at the expense of Englishmen, was that they should be butchered: hanged, but not until they were dead, cut open, their heart and bowels cast into the fire and their limbs distributed.

Tom Syddall died game. When his turn for the halter came he took a pinch of snuff, and hoped his children saw him die. As the hearts of each victim were cast into the fire, the hangman shouted 'God save King George,' and the Hanoverians with the Presbyterians cried, 'Amen.'

They stuck his head on the Manchester Exchange near to his own shop door, so that his wife could see it from her bedroom, where she was confined. Through all the trouble her sixth child came, and in her turn became a mother. Our precious mob, to celebrate Culloden, broke the windows of the widow. and frightened her away. The adherents of the Stuarts were all called Papists, who would 'spit, fire, burn and roast alive all heretics,' when they were only High Church Tories who believed in the right of the king in lineal descent to reign. If our king's are to be elected - be it so, but let us have Englishmen. The dull depression of the Georges weighed us down for generations.

'George the First was always reckonded
Vile – but viler George the Second.
And what mortal ever heard
Any good of George the Third?
When from earth the Fourth descended,
Heav'n be praised, the Georges ended.'

In my *Didisburye in the '45* I have given long extracts from the written statements delivered to the sheriff by the officers, before they were butchered, and a copy of Hogarth's picture of Temple Bar adorned with the heads of Colonel Townley and Captain Fletcher, and somebody's leg. It is not unlikely that leg would be one of Syddall's, for, as the adjutant of the regiment, he had been very active. He was described as a little man with a big nose; a peruke maker and barber by occupation, living in his own shop with his wife and five children. In those days it was the fashion to shave and to wear wigs.

There is an entry in the registers of Didsbury that I think refers to our hero: 'Oct. 1730. Thomas Siddall and Maria Fletcher de Burnage, and paroch Mancum conj matri per License. Rog. Bolton surr.' He would then be twenty-five years of age, and his wife may have been sister to Captain George Fletcher, who was a younger man supporting his mother. In 1745, the Court Leet records give Thomas Syddall and 'Mr. George ffletcher scavangers,' or, as we should now term it, 'on the sanitary committee.' The next year's Constables' Accounts solemnly record an expenditure of £00.01.06 'for tending the Sheriff the morn Syddall's and Deacon's heads put up.'

Whether any of Syddall's sons grew up and left sons I have never learnt. It is affecting to read in his last address how he thanked God for the example of an honest father, and prayed that his children might tread the same dangerous steps, and 'also have the courage and constancy to endure to the end, and despise Human Power when it stands opposed to Duty.'

Colonel Townley's skull I have handled from under the altar of the chapel in Townley Hall, where it was long preserved. A Captain Moss was one of the officers, but with the help of money, tools, and friends, he got out of Newgate with his friend Holker, and fled to France. I remember an old man at Didsbury named George Fletcher, who was christened after his uncle the 'Rebel', and it was whispered he was a rebel at heart, for he was a Chartist and a Radical. Jacobite Tories and Jacobin Radicals got mixed in the vulgar mind, but to call a man a Rebel and prophesy he would get 'bowelled' was something very terrible. To speak of him as a Martyr would be to court ostracism, and the brand of a madman or a dangerous Papist.

As an instance of two memories covering the hundred and fifty years after the famous '45', my great-grandmother, Nancy Fletcher, was born in 1729, remembered it, and was remembered by my mother up to 1900.

Opposite: The Porch and a further view of the entrance front

Soss Moss Hall

Under the fir-trees at Soss Moss we ate apples and sought for the black and white hall which stands close by the railway between Alderley and Chelford, of which several beautiful photographs were made. Its huge stone lichen-clothed chimney is signed and dated 'T Wyche, 1583'.

St Oswald's Church, Nether Peover

Speke is a wonderfully fine old black and white house of many gables enclosing spacious court-yard or quadrangle; a very difficult place to photograph for underneath the yews the shade is dense. Across the front there runs the plain inscription, 'This worke, 25 yards long, was wholly built by Edw. N. Esq. Ano. 1598'. The stone bridge is still intact but the moat is dry, transformed into a garden fair. One side of the great hall is panelled with lofty wainscoting carved in many compartments bearing the solemn warning, 'Slepe not till U hathe consederd how thow hathe spent ye day past If thow have well don thank God If othrways repent ye.' This panelling with the library was part of the sack of Holyrood in 1543 by Sir William Norres. Many specimens of armour and fine old chests are scattered around. Upstairs are quaint old bedsteads, carved and dated, one of 1583, with watch-pocket in the wood.

The floors are of clay, and the walls of wattle and daub. Many rooms look ghostly, with their time-worn, faded tapestry, and one grey lady in particular may at times be seen looking through the window down into the moat for the child heir of the house who once was drowned there. Perhaps she put him in and cannot rest. In Saint Raymund's room, where is his bed with name and arms, there should not be a ghost. On a window-sill I note a lodging-place for owls, and little boards are put to hold the swallows' nests. It is a charming, quaint, old, haunted house, and behind it is a grove of trees carpeted with hyacinthine blue in the spring, and beyond again is the sea, the estuary of the Mersey in its widest part, with a little worn-out pier, the ideal spot for smugglers and romance.

The view from the Moat

The courtyard

Tabley Old Hall, nr. Knutsford

According to Sir Peter Leycester, (the careful and painstaking pedigree recorder and historian of his part of Cheshire, who was born in the hall A.D. 1613), it was built about 1380. Most of the original building must have perished, but the central hall with its gallery and open stairway is probably the one then made with the readiest and best material they had, namely oak. The column as shown in the accompanying picture (p.132) is doubtless part of the original structure. The Jacobean mantelpiece is dated 1619. There are many scars and holes in the doors and panelling, which are said to have been made by spears or bullets or arrows, and the whole place, standing as it does in its little island home with only a chapel to keep it company, is very interesting.

The wild cherry-trees were laden with blossom, and the woods carpeted with anemones, not a single flower of which I touched. A water-hen croaked from the reeds, and a flash of light blue showed me that stately and picturesque bird, the heron, fishing by the water-side. As long as his dagger-like bill was pointed towards me he was almost invisible, but when he turned his head the pearly-grey breast and long crest-feathers were plainly seen. He flew off to his nest in the chestnut trees, and I thought of a distant piece of road from whence the heronry can be seen. The bird life was most abundant, and over all other sounds there constantly came the resonant trumpet-like note of the Canadian gander.

The garden front

One day about noon, when there was little traffic at Didsbury Station, a young porter whom I had not known came to me as I was waiting for a train, and touching his cap said, 'Have you ever photographed Tatton Old Hall, sir?' Being rather surprised, I answered hurriedly, 'I never heard of any old hall at Tatton, and don't think there is one.' His reply was, 'Oh yes there is, sir; I was born there.' 'Then you should know something about it – but where is it?' 'Down by the mere, sir, inside Tatton Park.'

This was very interesting, for I know as much about Cheshire as most men know, and yet I had never heard or read of any mention of Tatton Old Hall. The lad's information had all the ring of truth, for most of our old halls were moated or on islands in meres, and Tatton Park is an immense place, kept private most rigidly and religiously. It is said to be eleven miles round, containing twenty-five thousand acres, and has twenty-six locked gates. There is no mention of any old hall at Tatton in Ormerod's original great *History of Cheshire*. Its enlarger has put in a bit about the panelling of the dining-room in the present hall, which may be true if it refers to the panelling only, but not true if it refers to the room itself. On the ordnance map I found Tatton Old Hall was marked by the mere in the park as my informant had said, and I wrote to Earl Egerton of Tatton for permission to see over and photograph it.

The requisite permission was kindly sent at once, with a few historical notes by Lord Egerton, who was always interested in architecture and antiquities.

His lordship said the only part of architectural interest in what was left of the old hall of Tatton was in the timbers of the roof which were finely carved, and of the early part of the fifteenth century. They could only be photographed by the light from magnesium wire, and we must have the head game-keeper to watch us. It was rather a tedious job, for the attics under the roof were quite dark, and the beams were festooned with fishing nets hung up to dry. We could not stand upright, had to be careful about fire, and mind where we trod. The remainder of the present building has evidently been rebuilt from part of an older and larger hall. I think it had a courtyard, and was almost certainly on an island, for the land all round it, has evidently been under water for ages.

The head gamekeeper, a very big, fine-looking man, has the house shown [in part of the old hall]. One of his great mastiffs which was not in good health is standing by the door. There are two other lesser houses under the same roof; they are tenanted by servants on the estate: good gardens adjoin them, and the place looks well-kept and homely. It is thoroughly in the country, for there is not another house within a mile of it in the populous county of Cheshire. There may be a keeper's cottage or two hidden about the woods, but it seemed to me we tramped with our bicycles above a mile from Tatton Hall, across the rough grass of the park, often through swampy places where the peewits nest and the red deer watch from afar. We also tramped out on the Mobberley side of the park for a mile or so, before we could ride. We were escorted by a shepherd, who constantly told us the road to Ashley was 'as straight as a H'arrow' though he wound through woods and round corners and into farmyards in many devious tracks.

Having seen the old hall, and also the grand mansion known as the present hall, I wondered whether there had been any intermediate hall, and why there is no mention of them in history. It

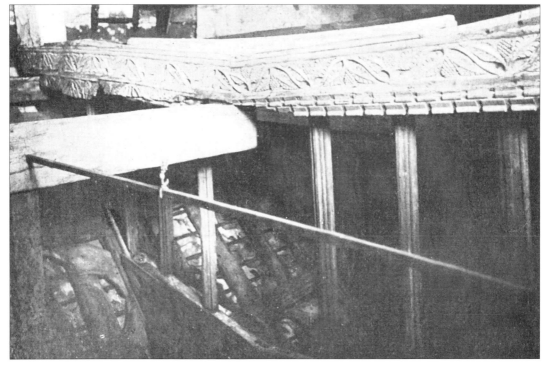

Old timbers in the roof

may be the old hall, being on an island in the mere in a remote and rather swampy part of Cheshire, would escape history, and for the greater part of two hundred years previous to the building of the present hall the owners of the estate lived elsewhere.

The Massys held Tatton for centuries. One of them fell at Shrewsbury fight on the side of Hotspur. The direct male line died about 1480 to 1490. In the female line the estates went to Stanleys and Breretons. In 1598 Richard Brereton of Tatton, Esquire, left Tatton to Thomas Egerton, the illegitimate half brother of his wife Dorothy, apparently acting on the principle of 'to him that hath much shall be given.' Thomas Egerton, Lord Chancellor of England, had acquired enormous estates elsewhere, for he had espoused the cause of the robbers of the lands of the religious houses, and had gotten almost endless land for himself in the time of its very greatest depression. He was buried at Dodleston, and his successors for three generations were buried at Little Gaddesden in Hertfordshire. It seems, therefore, they did not live in Cheshire, but as the family multiplied a branch came to Tatton, where Samuel Egerton, the last male, died in 1780. He was buried at Rostherne, and left the estates to his sister, Hester Tatton, and her issue, conditional on them taking the name of Egerton. Therefore, Egertons of Tatton they became, though Tattons of Tatton would have been nobler and truer. Hester Tatton's son, William Egerton, began to build the new hall at Tatton in 1794, and died before it was finished. Was it in the old hall his uncle, Sam Egerton, had died? The late Earl Egerton's letter to me says the old hall of Tatton was the seat of the Breretons; it does not say whether Egertons ever lived there, and we know they did not live there for at least a hundred years after they had the estate.

There happens to be a very curious little book with the title of *Family Anecdotes*, written by an Egerton who became the eighth Earl of Bridgewater. He was a thorough-bred parson, for his father and grandfather held many livings and became bishops. He was the Honourable and Reverend Francis Henry Egerton, who was proud of the picture of his natural daughter, and his perfumed poodles. He visited his kinsman, Sam Egerton, at Tatton, and mentions that his host had newly built and furnished a great room at Tatton, with a newly invented stove grate which a careless housemaid had spoilt. Also that Sam Egerton lost sixpence at backgammon, when he 'violently threw a crooked sixpence on the board, shrugged up his breeches, skuttled out of the room, and went fuming and fretting toward the lake, but cooling down, thought it was not worth while to drown himself for the loss of a sixpence at backgammon.'

From the above it would appear that Samuel Egerton, the first esquire of his name resident on the estate, built a great room from the old hall, and his nephew and successor began to build the present mansion.

It was amusing to me to find there was a youth working on the railway who knew something of my work, and could tell me a bit of history that all our local historians had missed. He must have been reading and watching me while I had never seen him.

Old Tatton Hall in Tatton Park

Wardley Hall, Swinton, Lancashire

During our conversation with the Benedictine Dom at Baddesley Clinton we had promised to send him a photograph of the skull of Father Ambrose if we could get the requisite permission, and I said, at the same time, there would be less doubt about the permission than about our ability to obtain a good photograph; for I knew the skull was kept in a hole in the wall on the staircase, with fixed glass in front of it. There was very great difficulty in focussing, for with all our best spectacles on there was little or nothing to see in the camera but the reflection of the light, from off the glass. X prepared me for the worst and then brought out a good photograph, as he has often done before and since.

This is the only pilgrimage we have ever made without our bicycles; but as we were going through a squalid suburb of the city, it was more prudent to leave them behind. The reader shall not be troubled with any description of the miserable grimy streets of Salford. In a few miles we came to higher ground, with fewer houses, but the people were no cleaner. A badly worn paved road led through a blackened land dotted with coal-pits, or mills, overhung with a dull pall of smoke, through which the shrieking engines and the clanging trains rushed on their hideous way. It was no use trying to think that this wretchedness and wealth were synonymous. The abomination of desolation brooded over all, but an end came to our depression when we turned a corner and suddenly found ourselves before a bit from another century or another country, standing alone as if it were forgotten and forlorn.

In a secluded nook in the bare low hills, partly hidden by trees that are struggling for life and environed by the water of a moat on which wild ducks are tamely resting, trying to uphold the air of sport and respectable antiquity stands Wardley Hall, the house of the skull. Like all the old houses it has been built and rebuilt at many times and on the ruins of many that have gone before it. Wherever there was an island, or a peninsula that could be made into an island, and on which a dwelling could be built, there our earliest forefathers would be certain to make their home. Because that home was so safe, not only in the petty wars that went on all down the long ages, but in times of peace when any dark winter's night might bring some dangerous guests. With draw-bridge pulled up the outer world was shut away, and within the 19th century there was no access to Wardley Hall but by a bridge that ended at a door. The drawing made by N. G. Philips in 1822 shows the gatehouse as a timber-framed building with high-pitched roof having other buildings of various dates and styles on either side of it that rise from the edge of the water. There was more black-and-white work when I first saw it than there is now, for, like many of the old manor-houses, it had decayed into being a farmhouse with labourers cottages, but now all has been restored and reconverted into a gentleman's residence.

There were three generations of the Downes family who lived at Wardley, and as all the histories, true and untrue, connect them with the skull, I will try to disentangle and make plain the facts. From their conversions and perversions the family seem to have been rather eccentric. The first Roger married, twice, Catholic wives and embraced their religion. The second Roger died young. The third was brought up in the English Church, but was no credit to it. His mother was a daughter of Sir Cecil Trafford of Trafford, who was a Protestant. Sir Cecil argued so much about religion with the first Roger that he himself converted to Romanism; that is instead of 'um converting um, um converted um.' In my younger days we were delighted with the arithmetic and algebra of Colenso. Then we heard the great man was made a bishop and had gone to convert the heathen. The next tale was that he applied his arithmetic to the measurements of Noah's ark; found that all the animals from the elephant to the kangaroo could not possibly be

136

The garden front

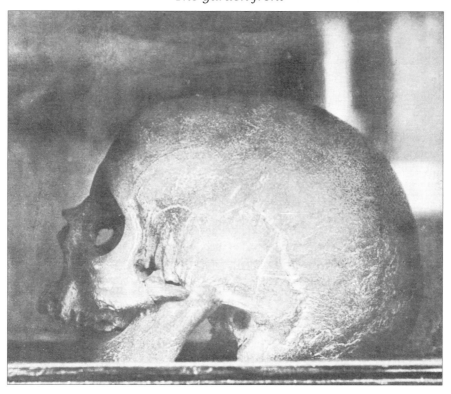

The skull of Edward Barlow (Father Ambrose, The Order of St Benedictine)

got into it; and finally the Kaffirs converted him. Great are the powers of arithmetic!

The histories generally say the skull at Wardley is that of Roger Downes, alluding to the third of the name. He was the son of John Downes and Penelope Trafford, his father dying when be was very young. As he grew to manhood he became what was then termed a rake or roysterer. It is said the name 'rake' was given to those who, if they saw the reflection of the moon in water, would rake for it, or for anything else. He was in a drunken brawl at Epsom Wells and was killed at the age of twenty-eight. With some friends he was having what is now called a 'lark' or 'spree.' They were tossing some fiddlers in a blanket for not fiddling as they were ordered. Then they broke the constable's head.

'Ye constable cried out murther and one of ye watch came behind Mr. Downs and with a spittle staff cleft his scull. Ye Lord Rochester and ye rest ran away and Mr. Downs having noe sword snatched up a sticke and strikinge at them they run him into ye side with a half pike and soe bruised his arme yt he wase never able to stir it after.' It could not matter much about bruising his arm if his skull was cleft and he had a half pike in his side. They brought him home and buried him at Wigan, doubtless with all solemn pomp and in the full odour of sanctity. His head was said to be kept at Wardley. Then, in after years, there were doubts about this head. Other lords or squires came into possession of the estate and did not want to have an old skull knocking about. But they had to keep it. They opened Roger's grave to make sure about him, and found his head was fast to his skeleton all right, excepting a bit that had evidently been chipped off the top. Whose, then, was the famous skull? If anything was done to it, or it was not treated with proper respect, such commotions arose about the house that no one dare live in it. Windows were blown in, cattle pined in the stall, and the things were bewitched.

A friend of mine, who was shooting by the side of the moat, saw a rabbit rise up from below the water, swim across, and disappear, he being too scared to shoot. It might have been a hare or a cat, as those uncanny beasts were always connected with witchcraft, and there was only its head to see. If that had been shot the skull would have been injured. Some reckless scapegrace once threw the skull into the moat to be rid of it, but all the water had to be drained off and the treasure restored, while countless troubles haunted him. There is plenty of testimony to the ill luck that has happened when the skull has been disturbed, This has not come from the superstitious only, but from shrewd, observant men of business, whose word is as good as their bond, and whose truthfulness is fully equal to, or rather better than, that of the average man, including lawyers and parsons.

In this age of agnosticism it is as well to record another instance in this neighbourhood of disturbance to a skull bringing ill luck to all around. At Tunsted, near Chapel-en-le-Frith, which is about twenty miles east from Didsbury, there is a similar relic which was so shocked at the profanity of the navvies who were making a line of railway from Whaleybridge to Buxton, that it sunk or blasted their work as fast as it was done, and the contractors deviated the line to escape from its sphere of influence. All the powers of steam and science were mocked by the refusal of the navvies to endure the ill luck and to work under the ban of 'old Dicky's' skull. This also is in my lifetime and neighbourhood.

I believe the skull at Wardley to be that of Edward Barlow, of whom I wrote under Barlow Hall. Although it is only three years since that was written [in 1903] another change has come; the district has amalgamated with the neighbouring city, and Barlow Hall is now in the Didsbury ward of the city of Manchester.

Wardley Hall in 1876

The same view 30 years later

In the Didsbury Church registers there is still in existence the entry or record of the baptism on the thirtieth of November.

FACSIMILE OF ENTRY

The Barlows of Barlow were a long-settled family who kept to their old faith at the time of the Reformation. On the sundial and on the chapel window of the present house is the date 1574. Ten years after this rebuilding the house was searched for priests, and the master, who was ill, taken to prison in Manchester. It is said that he 'verted his custodian, but he soon died and was buried within a few yards of where I write. He was the grandfather of Edward. His son was also called Alexander, and became a knight. He had been married at four years old; renounced that child-wife, and married Mary, the daughter of Sir Uryan Brereton of Honford, now called Handforth, a fine old black-and-white hall five miles south of Didsbury,

Edward Barlow became Father Ambrose, a Benedictine, and acted as a priest in the Roman Catholic Church when it was unlawful to do so in England. On Easter Day 1641 as he was preaching at Morleys Hall, 'a neighbouring minister,' probably from Eccles or Leigh, in his sur-plice and with a mob arrested him, ransacked the house without warrant, and sent him with armed escort to Lancaster Gaol; that is, they left their own devotions to stop the other fellow's. 'The better the day the better the deed' parsons will tell you when it suits them. On Easter Day 1871 the bishop was to preach at Didsbury, and I, as churchwarden, was standing by the church door before service when a stranger came and bought a sitting of game-fowl eggs, for which he paid me five shillings. I told the rector, who was shocked at trading on the Sabbath, but thought the best thing to do was to put the money in the collection. So the man got the eggs; the Church got the money, and I got absolution – all at the joyous Eastertide.

Barlow was tried at the Assizes for being a Romish priest when the king had commanded all priests to depart the realm. This shifty king, or Sacred Majesty, with all his progeny, had to rely mainly on the Catholics when they were in trouble. Careless and faithless, their turn came. The judge argued with the priest and told him of his power; but Barlow, acknowledging himself to be a priest, replied: 'If my lord, in consequence of so unjust a law, you should condemn me to die, you would send me to heaven and yourself to hell.' It vexes lawyers to be told they will go to hell, for there are doubts about there being such a place for anybody. Barlow was sentenced to be hanged, drawn, quartered, and boiled in tar. How the neighbouring 'ministers,' strong in the 'odium theologicum,' would enjoy the spectacle! They followed him, as he was dragged on a hurdle to the gallows, trying to convert him, and doubtless thanked God that they themselves were of sound doctrine. I wonder whether they wore their surplices for the ceremony.

The martyr's head would be impaled on high where he was taken, or on the nearest place of Christian worship. Morleys Hall is about five miles from Wardley, the Tyldesley family having owned both places. Francis Downes, son of the first Roger and uncle to the third, was then the Lord of Wardley. He was a strong Catholic, and is believed to have rescued the head of Barlow. The tale of it being the head of Roger was probably spread to throw the relic-hunters off the scent. Sir Alexander, the brother of Edward Barlow appointed 'my lovinge cosen Roger Downes of Wardley esquier Vice chainberlaine of the countie pallatyne of Chester to bee overseer' of his will. Roger died before either of the Barlows; but they were evidently related, and the relic treasured by Roger's heir. The wonder is, how has it been preserved through all these years of indifference and unbelief and surrounded by coal pits?

There are more skulls in our old halls than the ordinary mortal knows. Englishmen do not like to parade the skeleton in the cupboard. Perhaps the first genuine pilgrimage I ever made was to Townley Hall to see the head of Colonel Townley who was executed with Captain Fletcher in the '45. At first, I was told, it was not there – they knew nothing about it; but after some little talk the butler told me it was under the altar in the private chapel, and I carefully handled and examined it. The teeth were perfect, excepting the two front ones, they having probably been taken to wear as a charm against toothache by some philosopher.

At Browsholme in Bowland, where the family of Parkers have dwelt for centuries, there is an ancient skull, but none of a party of antiquaries could tell anything about it. A medical man thought it had been a woman's, and priests were present, but nothing was told us. A notable relic in the house is the stirrup or dog gauge through which all dogs in the Forest of Bowland had to pass.

Here are a few thoughts from the solitude of a dreamer on the dreamless head of Barlow. We have most of us heard or read of martyrs. Many of the tales are sadly lacking in realism or apparent truth but when a case occurs among our own people, and in our own neighbourhood, it certainly does come home to us. A short walk from this Old Parsonage, Didsbury, down the meadows by the banks of the river Mersey, takes one to Barlow Hall, where, in country phrase, Edward Barlow was bred, born, and reared. Rooms he lived in are there now. Within a few yards of where this is written he was baptized and the kindred of the Barlows lie; the family had given priests to this church of Didsbury centuries before. The names of the scenes and of the actors in the dark tragedy are familiar to us. There are today men of the name and lineage of Barlow of Barlow toiling as day labourers on the land which bears their name and of which their fathers once were lords. In our public life today we meet men whom we may know and work with for years without knowing of what sect they are or what creed, if any, they profess.

Education or indifference increases mutual toleration. To learn how 'these Christians love one another,' go to church or mix in the affairs of the Church. As it was in the beginning it is now. At the great festival of the Christian's year, Easter (not the Passover), Barlow was arrested without warrant, in a private house, by a mob headed by a rival priest in his surplice. Apparently this rival priest wore his sacerdotal vestment to show that he was doing the work of the Lord on His Holy day and needed not the sanction or help of the law. They brought no accusation against him, excepting the one that he was a Romish priest – which he acknowledged.

He was a hard-working, frugal ascetic, who would not look at a woman and abstained from flesh and wine, for he said 'wine and women make the wise apostatise.' If he had done endless rapes and murders he could not have been condemned to a more horrible death than the priests and lawyers forced on him. Milton's 'two-handed engine' had to smite more than once to quarter the body before it was thrown in the boiling tar. A fringe of dark chestnut hair escaped even that until recent years.

'This skull had a tongue in it, and could sing once.' Even on the gallows it was heard in the 'Miserere' ere it was hushed in death.

All this happened in our little corner of Merry England two hundred and sixty-four years ago. The time is short, but the changes are man. They are many even in my time – what will they be in another century or two?

The Hall, Lake and Boat house

The top of the stairs

The staircase showing where the skull is fixed

Welltrough Hall, Withington

Welltrough or Wheltrough is a picturesque house on a hill, with part of the moat still in existence and on the side of the hill. If this is the hill in this neighbourhood called Tunsted which I have read about, its name alone denotes great antiquity.

Across the fields to the left of The Bents (see page 38), over the river by a wooden plat bridge and up the hill, is Woodford Old Hall, ornate with quatrefoils of black and white, and overhanging upper storeys on its northern side. Like so many other ancient houses, it has perished and gone on its southern or weather-beaten side and rebuilt ugly and common. Its age can only be guessed, but it is very great, as the new hall to which we are going is dated 1630, and this one, as its name imports, must have been old before the new was built. The big barn has the initials "I. D." for John Davenport, and 1660. The guardian yew tree is there. We walk through fields to find our way to Woodford New Hall.

Woodford New Hall was built of stone and brick, for we are getting nearer to the stone country of the hills. Over its portal is the date with the initials and arms of the Davenports, members of the once all-powerful family in the Forest of Macclesfield who owned the estate then and own it now. One room is panelled in oak. The oaken beams are carved, and on the tiny panes of glass are relics of revelry where, it may be, the fear of the future haunted the feast even as a spectre. For, nearly two hundred years ago, the Davenports and their neighbours, the Leghs, of Adlington, scratched their names on the little diamond-shaped panes of glass in the window, and one wrote: 'Long live good company' and women wrote: 'Heaven long preserve us both.' Whether these women wished to be preserved in heaven or on the earth they did not say; let them have the benefit of any doubt.

Worsley Old Hall, Worsley

There is an old Hall within about a dozen miles of my home, that is worthy of being recorded among our historic homes. It was hatched a scheme for great works which were constructed under great difficulties, and in the wear and tear of time have proved to be of inestimable good to millions of our countrymen and have never been of harm to any one.

About a hundred and fifty years ago circumstances drove a young duke, the third Duke of Bridgewater – (a good name for him) to a solitary, dreamy life where he would not be troubled with women, and in retirement at Worsley Hall, near to the coalpits of Lancashire and by the sterile waste of Chat Moss. He lived laborious days, spending his wealth in planning and scheming how to cheapen the carriage of the coal that was plentiful under his estates, to the ever-increasing population of the neighbouring towns. They were often starving for lack of fuel while around him it could be had for the digging.

The first Duke of Bridgewater's fifth son succeeded to his titles and estates in his twelfth year. Like his elder brothers, he was a sickly child, who was thought to be weak in body and mind. Neglected by his mother, he was fortunately left to himself and servants. Naturally he would ride on horseback, play skittles, travel, fall in love, and in his green youth was nearly captured by a beautiful young widow, the Duchess of Hamilton, who as Miss Gunning had been married at midnight with a ring of the bed curtain, and was soon on the look-out for another duke as husband. In the nick of time there was a lucky quarrel, and the youth took fright, vowing never to trust a woman again. He shunned the society of all women, and forbade them his house; in homely phrase, petticoats became an abhorrence to him. He took temporary refuge in snuff, but in work – thoughtful, active, never-ending work – he found his reward and his consolation.

Hidden away beneath the earth of Worsley were fields of coal, inexhaustible mines of black diamonds that were indeed 'a potentiality of wealth beyond the dreams of avarice'; but the only means of getting the coal to those who needed it was by pack-horses trudging with heavy loads on their backs along the bad roads, or by men lugging and tugging narrow boatloads along the rivers and watercourses. The cost of carrying the coal to Manchester was then as much as the cost of the coal at the pit's mouth at Worsley. It might be more, for if a horseload, or two hundred-weight, cost tenpence at Worsley, it would probably cost more than that in freight; and in severe winters, when the coal was most needed, the whole traffic was stopped.

In 1757 the population of Manchester and Salford was twenty thousand, and there was a famine in the land. Folk were 'welly clemmed,' their food was 'nobbut' oatmeal or barleymeal, and fuel could hardly be gotten: starvation stared them in the face, and the poor children shivered in misery and want. Dr. Byrom wrote a famous skit:

'Bone and Skin,
Two millers thin,
Would starve us all or near it.
But be it known
To Skin and Bone
That Flesh and Blood can't bear it.'

It referred to a doctor and a barrister, who were trustees of the charity school and farmers of the town mills. They were literally skinny men in their persons and in their stinginess. Bone was Dawson, a doctor or 'sawbones,' and father of Jemmy Dawson, an officer in the Manchester

Worsley Old Hall

Regiment who was executed for his share in the '45, and whose sweetheart, Katherine Norton, would see the end of him, saw it, and died on the spot. Skin was Joseph Yates, a barrister, whose son, Sir Joseph Yates, became a Justice of the King's Bench and Common Pleas. Law seems to be bred in their skin for the fourth of the name and the profession is Joseph Maghull Yates, K.C., the Chairman of our Quarter Sessions, with whom I have the honour and pleasure of sitting, and he is not the last of his name and learning.

I and my forbears have only had sorrow with law and next to nothing with doctors, but have always had their business among the food of the people, who never would believe a miller could be honest unless he had a tuft of hair growing in the palm of his hand. In times of scarcity the poor naturally became ravenous, and blamed any one who sold or who had food. Nowadays we have no conception of the misery and famine that every wet summer brought to this damp part of England. In wet harvests, wheat cannot ripen, or it sprouts after ripening: then the flour from it will not rise (or be leavened) and bread cannot be baked.

It was easy for the Duke to see that if he could by any means have his coal sent cheaply to Manchester there was an enormous fortune for him and great good to his poor neighbours. He and his land agent John Gilbert talked it over and over again at Worsley Hall; there was no doubt that carriage by water was cheaper than by any other means, but how could the waterway be made? In their dilemma they fortunately sent for a millwright or mechanic they had heard of, and James Brindley, a born genius, appeared on the scene.

Brindley had been born in a poor cottage on the barren hills called the Peak of Derbyshire, [at Wormhill, near Tideswell] where it is difficult for anything to live long and wonderful that any really good thing should be produced. He was said to be a stupid lad, but his mother made the best of him she could, and at seventeen years old he bound himself prentice to a drunken millwright at Sutton near Macclesfield. Brindley had no schooling, and his mechanical knowledge came 'natural like.' At twenty-six he started business at Leek as a wheelwright, and charged two shillings a day for his labour'.

In 1759, Brindley came to Worsley Hall and made an 'ochilor ricconitoring,' as he wrote of his ocular survey of the ground. His plan was to cut a canal or navigable trench on the level, independent of all streams of water, and to make it watertight by puddling. The Duke believed in him, and applied to Parliament for the requisite powers to acquire the land.

The greatest difficulty that had to be overcome was the carrying of the canal on the level on an embankment over the low lands near to the Irwell by a bridge and over the river itself, so as not to interfere with its navigation. Brindley got over this by the famous aqueduct at Barton, that was then looked upon as one of the wonders of the world. This 'building of castles in the air' was ridiculed by every one when being constructed, and it must have tested the power of will and the steady faith of both master and man in the long, anxious time of its trial.

This 'dream of a madman' lasted as sound as when it was finished for about one hundred and forty years, when it was taken down for the construction of the Manchester Ship Canal, and a swinging aqueduct was substituted for it. The scientific men of the day laughed at the canal in the air, and the common folk said, 'That ere Brindley's a ruinin' o' th' Duke.'

But the Duke was not easily ruined. He had vast estates and great tenacity of purpose. He devoted his life's work to making a way for his inexhaustible stores of coal to be cheaply carried to his neighbours' doors, and in that he was wonderfully helped by the 'unlettered peasant,' the innate genius whom he employed, and who began his day's work in the good old-fashioned manner by drinking a bowl of milk.

At Worsley Hall they sat up till far into the night scheming, planning, arguing, sometimes quarrelling, until they were worn out, and had to rest as well as they could and begin again. Ready money soon got spent, and the chief work of Gilbert the agent became the borrowing of loans

Detail of the Hall

from the tenantry or from any one who would advance £5 or upwards.

There was nothing spent unnecessarily. The Duke limited himself to £400 a year, including the keep of two horses and a groom; and as there were no women servants at the Hall, I suppose the groom was chambermaid and maid of all work. But who did the cooking? Perhaps there was none, or the Duke did it himself. Brindley got a guinea a week for wages, and he could not well keep a groom out of that, though he also lived at the Hall and rode 'a hors bak' sometimes. He charged sixpence a day for 'ating and drink' when he was off 'countin caridgos' or seeing 'the engon at woork.' For going to London 'on hors bak' and back again, with eight days in the city, he charged £4. 8s. 0d. for 'self and hors and all expences.' The travelling either way would take four or five days, and no Scotchman would have done it for the money, but he was Derbyshire bred and skinny.

Once, but only once, he went to a theatre; it was to see *Richard III* played by Garrick. He vowed he would never go again, for it made him ill, and he had to give evidence before the Lords and Commons. He astonished those gentlemen by his manners and language, and as their untutored intellects could not understand his mechanics, he had to give them 'ochilor' demonstrations. He brought a cheese and cut it up for them as a model of his aqueduct at Barton, and some clay to puddle, trying to show them how a canal could be made watertight by puddled clay. Puddling was his great panacea for all evils in canaldom, and it is written that almost his last words when he was dying were, 'Puddle it, puddle it.'

Brindley's influence and credit appear to have steadily increased, though he had his 'werrets.' When the land agent wished to show his superior position Brindley wrote a short note to him, 'no more sosity'; and when the Tories raged against his bill in Parliament he made a note, 'The Toores mad had agane ye Duk,' for the sacred land must not be meddled with even by a Duke who had many broad lands of his own, and was one of a family noted for sticking to them and adding to them.

The tale that is best known in the neighbourhood of Brindley's many original dodges is of the clock that strikes thirteen, for the clock itself still testifies to the truth of the tale. The workmen at Worsley were ready enough to drop their tools when the clock struck twelve, but not to begin work again at one. Their excuse was that as the clock only struck once they might miss hearing it, it was so different to hearing twelve hammered into them. So in future when one o'clock came thirteen strokes unfeelingly prolonged the din.

Half-crown Row took its name, as the colliers say, because 'Tould dook foined ony mon as didner gor dawn th' pit o' Moonday morn auve a crawn': and it is presumed he built a row of houses with the spare money they would have spent in drink. The Duke himself would be certain to become more penurious during his long struggle with poverty, or rather with the want of ready money to pay his workmen and other expenses incurred in the construction of the canal, for he never would sell or mortgage any of his estates. He would not allow the growing of such useless things as flowers, and became so nervous about the weather when some of his works were in progress, that every few minutes he would rush off to stir up the barometer.

'Patience and perseverance overcome difficulties' the Duke and Brindley knew that, though they knew not copybook maxims. Steadily they stuck to their task, unflinchingly mastering every detail, and the canal was finished. Miles of underground waterways drained the coalpits of their water, and in long, narrow, deep boats on the water floated down the coal into the basin of Worsley, where the water supplied all that was needed for the canal independently of rain or rivers. No amount of traffic wears the water out, and when the coal first came to Manchester, its price was dropped to one-half what it had ever been before. In fact the Duke had bound himself, when giving evidence for his Act of Parliament, that his coal should be sold in Manchester at not more than 4d. for 120 lbs., and the men of Manchester drank and shouted for joy.

The canal from Worsley to Manchester, with its branch to Runcorn, is said to have cost £220,000, and soon to have paid £80,000 a year. Brindley planned and made it for a daily wage of half-a-crown for part of the time and a guinea a week for some of the time. He never spent a penny he could help, and that also well pleased the parsimony of the Duke who must have been unpleasant to live with. His cousin, the eighth Earl of Bridgewater, wrote that he had lived with him in his house for ten years, and found him to be a domestic tyrant, selfish in all things, regardless of duties to relatives, giving nothing in charity, and never attending any place of public worship. That opinion may be considerably discounted, for his cousin was 'crabbed' because the Duke had cut off the entail of the estates and left him nothing. If the Duke did not attend public worship he did better than his cousin, a parson who circulated the picture of Sophia Cotton, his natural daughter, with the statement under it that she was his natural daughter. He was the Honourable and Reverend Francis Henry Egerton, the son of a bishop and 'L'Ami du Pauvre,' though every one of his poodle dogs had a valet to dress it and wait on it at table.

The reader may be wondering what has all this to do with Worsley Hall and our pilgrimage. The explanation is that in the old Hall at Worsley was hatched and fostered knowledge that the enormous advantages to be gained by the carriage of heavy goods by water could be extended and made possible all over the country by the extension of canals, or inland navigation independent of rivers or natural streams. The enormous profits made by the Duke's trustees after his death increased. Something had to be done with the money, and by way of spending a little of it, £100,000 was taken to build a grand new Hall at Worsley The old home of which I write became Worsley Old Hall.

The Duke kept his claws on the canal and the estates as long as he could even after his death, for he tied everything up as strictly as possible during the lifetime of every one he knew, and for twenty years after the death of all of them. He could not do more, and his great-nephew, Lord Francis Leveson Gower, who was three years old at the Duke's death, succeeded to the income, and became the first Earl of Ellesmere.

The inheritors of the land and the 'black diamonds' got the wealth. Brindley got precious little: his widow in her poverty petitioned for something in addition to a balance due to Brindley at the time of his death. He had said that seven years wages were due to him besides some travelling expenses, but all the widow appears to have received was £100.

It is also stated that the Duke bequeathed about £600,000 in legacies. The canals, with their quays, warehouses, &c., were sold in 1872 to the Bridgewater Navigation Company for £1,120,000, and resold by them, thirteen years after, to the Manchester Ship Canal Company for £1,710,000.

A big share of the half-million profit made so easily by the Bridgewater Navigation Company was spent in law, but the previous lump made by the Bridgewater Trustees went to the Earls of Ellesmere.

It surprised me greatly, when writing in my last book about Hall i th' Wood, to find cotton-spinning had crept into the accounts of our pilgrimages, and now the surprise is intensified to find myself wandering off in a pilgrimage to 'the Duke's' home, to be writing about the Duke's canals, by which, in my young days, we brought hundreds of thousands of tons of oats and oatmeal from Ireland, of flour from France and Spain, and in later years of corn from America and flour from Austria. It was in the early 'sixties' of the last century [i.e., 1860s] that I took a more active interest in my father's business of a corn merchant, and well do I remember being taken through the Duke's warehouses to see the big stocks my father had there piled up, for he speculated heavily, regardless of the forces against him. There were about twenty thousand sacks of Spanish flour that cost over fifty shillings a sack, which were kept for years till the bags rotted and the meal-worms flourished, and then were sold at thirty shillings the sack, the worms being given in, as the weevils were with the beans. Oats from the Emerald Isle came up the canal in ship-loads, were shot into bins – that is, were spread on the floors of big rooms – and there they were left till they sprouted and grew luxuriantly, green blades like grass, that used up the kernel of the damp oats, losing heavily in weight and wasting the goodness and the worth. Nearly all that trade is dead: oatmeal, that used to be largely the food of the people, is now sold in little packets, and the imports of wheat to be made into flour at the port are ever increasing, while in the little mills in the country the grinding of wheat has ceased.

About Christmas time the farmers often sent us presents of geese or turkeys with their cheese, and sometimes these would be frozen up in the canal. I think it would be the winter of the Crimean War that we had several frozen fast in the ice. We had expected 'Dicky Simpson's goose' for a Sunday before Christmas, but it did not come until the holidays were over and we had gone back to school, having talked for six weeks about that goose.

I still buy my coal from 'the Duke's,' as his trustees were called before the inheritance came to the Earl of Ellesmere. The price does exceed the 4d. per 120 lbs. they were bound not to exceed.

It is now 1s. $0^1/_2$d for 112 lbs., and no doubt they would say it must be dearer because rates and taxes are higher. But so are mine. It is good coal, burning steadily away with very little ash. It is tumbled into the boats at Worsley, miles from the light of day, floated to Stretford, carted here, gives a cheerful warmth, and his Lordship allows me $3^1/_2$d. out of the sovereign if I pay in a week: and a contented mind is great riches.

Worsley Old Hall

Worsley with coal boats on the river

Wrinehill Park

I well remember my father showing me an old house near to a large pool below the railway viaduct at Betley and saying that was Wrinehill Hall. Many things happen in fifty years. I had never found my way there, and was not very likely to find it, for there is only a cart-track for nearly half a mile, and underneath the railway the slutch would be six inches deep. Pilgrims suffer hardships gladly – if they get their reward, and we were not much disappointed. We found an enormous farm yard with a venerable gateway in the middle. On the other side of a large pool of water, that is fringed with reeds and less than it was in days gone by, there is a small mill and a big house not very old. I could not make the gateway fit the house for the breadth of the pool was between them. The farmer came to see what we were after, so I asked him if we might photograph the stone columns. His reply was something like, 'Oh aye, but what's the good of fortygraffink them things, they're nobbut owd rubbitch. One o' them stone balls fell a bit sin and did mak' such a hole i' th' muck. If yo wanten some ut to fortygraf, tak' ma young bull – that would be a pictur' – he's a bonny beast – he is so. Pedigree bred? Rather! Twelve months old last Valentine's Day middle o' th' neet.'

We learnt that only a few years since there stood by this gateway two enormous walnut trees. One was struck by lightning and the other felled as some one offered £7.10s.0d for it. But after it had been felled it was found to be not sound in the heart, and the buyer 'rued bargain and wouldn'r a' it.' The old hall has utterly vanished. Our new friend told us he had ploughed its site and set it with potatoes. Fancy the dust of the knightly families of Hawkstones and Egertons becoming potatoes! It may be the best use that could be made of it.

The rent notes for the estate are in the name of the Earl of Wilton 'and others,' and the descent of the estate as shown by the Egerton pedigree is rather interesting.

The great-grandson of Sir John Hawkstone was Hugh de Eggerton of Wrynhill, Esquire, who built himself a new Hall on the small estate (elsewhere named the Wryne or Wrineford). The Egertons stuck to the place with the tenacity of the family, and about two hundred years after Hugh, Sir John Egerton of Wrinehill married an heiress, Elizabeth Holland of Heaton and Denton, near Manchester. Sir John died at Wrinehill, but his progeny built Heaton Hall and his great-grandson was the first Earl of Wilton.

All that is left of Wrinehill Hall

Above: The Dower House

Church's Mansion

Nantwich

For five hundred years Nantwich had two names, Wich being the chief part of each of them. It was Wich Malbanck in aristocratic circles and official deeds, but with the common folk the old British name ultimately won. Domesday says there was 'unum Wich in quo erat puteus ad sal faciendum et ibi erant viii Salinae' (' one Wich in which there was a well for making salt, and there were eight salthouses'). The Norman scribes had their Latin words for well, salt, and salthouses where the salt was made, but Wich for an overflowing well of salt water had no equivalent in their language, though it had been locally used for centuries. It is very unlikely the British word Nant would be tacked on to a word in a later language.

Like the boiling over of the brine, this screed has been wrought by the overflow of bile at the sound of Namptwyche for Nantwich. Let the affectation go, as Wich Malbanck or Malbedeng has gone.

In the Hospital Street of the old town we tarried to take photographs of the old house here shown. Its name is rather interesting; the old-fashioned natives will tell you it is Church's Mansion, and must not be called Church house. There was a Church House once, but probably it got burnt in one of the numerous fires that devastated the picturesque, timber-framed, thatched houses of Nantwich, for a Richard del Churchehouse is the first form of the name. In 1474 John and Nicholas Churchehouse bought land, buildings, gardens, and orchards in 'Hospitull strete,' and a hundred years afterwards Richard Church built the fine old house we see.

James Hall, who wrote the history of Nantwich and whom I remember, was a careful scribe, and he gave the inscription on the house beginning 'Rycharde Churche and Margerye Churche.' In the photograph by X it appears to me to be 'Richard and Margaret,' so probably there has been some 'restoration.'

'Rycharde Churche and Margerye Churche his wyfe Mai iiii Thomas Clease made this worke anno dni mccccclxxvii in the xviiij yeare of the reane of our noble queene elesabeth.'

Hall gives some other inscriptions that we did not see, for we were not allowed to enter unless we would take 'Apartments,' as cleaning or something was going on inside.

'The roote of Wysdom is to Feare God
and the branch thereof shall too endure.'

Inside an old cupboard:

'Blessed art thov that feares and wallkest in his wayes
For thov shalte eate and happie arte.'

These inscriptions are probably the work of the builder, Thomas Cleese, who left his name and mottoes elsewhere. Here is another that had been long hidden under coats of plaster on the oak:

'A Bewtifvl face is a Dvmbe prais Faire women
be davngerovs markes for yong mans eyes
Choose not thy wife by hir bewty bvt by hir honesty.'

How are the young man's eyes to see her honesty?

A common name in the Church family was Saboth, for the family, like most of the good people of Nantwich, were rather puritanical in the time of the Civil War. It was here that 'the Clerk to the Council, John Bostocke of Tatnall Esquire, Learned in the Lawes was taken in the vicarage howse in the Acte of Adultery with one Alice Chetwood upon the Sabothe daye att tyme of Dyvyne servis and adiudged 'to stand in the markett place vpon the markett daye with papers signifyinge his sin vpon 'his Brest' and with her. It was known that 'Moses in the law commanded such should be stoned,' and the pair with the condemnation on them were set in the cage in the market-place on the market day for the stoning or the gaze of all. What happened beforetime happened again; there was no one without sin in Nantwich to cast the first stone. That was on Saturday the seventeenth of June 1643, further particulars being given by an eye-witness, Malbon, a descendant of the family whose name the place had borne, and whose diary is the most interest-ing account of the Civil War for miles round Nantwich that has been written.

Richard Church, who built the house, was probably a descendant of the Churchehouse who bought the land, and of the still earlier Richard of the Churchehouse. From the length of his will he was a wealthy man who had made money out of the local salt trade. He died in 1592, leaving to Margery, his widow, 'occupation of salt for forty years if she live soe long.' To his son William 'one Wiche house of six leads in Wich Malbank,' with other property. The name of Wich Malbank was used in documents later than this. Rondull, the second son, had 'the house wherein I now dwell in Ospell Street' and five Wiche houses in Middlewich. Rondull lived at the ' Mansion to a great age, dying in 1648, when another branch of the Church family succeeded him.

Eight generations were named Saboth, or Sabbath. They were not all born in wedlock and I find one married a Martha Moss. I never heard of her before, but the history also relates that a Peter Moss was fined for being drunk and using abusive language to the tenant of the Church Mansion. Probably he was a relation of Martha and her children, and thought the paltry accident of some Church not being churched ought not to interfere with their rights to the property, and some day he would be primed to give everybody a bit of his mind.

When Hall wrote his history, nearly thirty years since the Saboth Churches had gone to Canada the old house being owned by the Radford-Norcops of Betton, who were descendants of the builder. Though the male line had faded twice. In 1691 Mr. Churche's house and orchard were rated at two shillings and eight pence halfpenny, leaving plenty of room for the rates to go up. In recent years it became a lawyer's office, and it took ten years of fresh air and emptiness to recover from that. It was then a young ladies' seminary or as an old servant of ours would always say: 'a cemetery' for young ladies. When we were there Apartments 'were to let' and the landlady did not like the look of us.

Fletcher Moss published this photograph with the caption "a doomed bit of Cheshire". Its location is unknown, but perhaps a local reader can place it from an indentification of the church.
This volume is to be followed by one on the Welsh Borders, so if it can be indentified, its location will be given in that book!

Acknowledgements

The publishers would like to thank Josephine Chaloner, Eunice Roberts, Manchester & Wrexham Central Libraries for assistance in the production of this book.

Other books in the Landmark Collector's Series

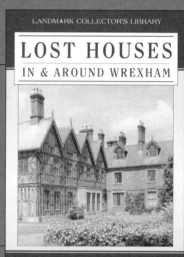